From

Roger NG.

June 1977

Musical Thoughts & Afterthoughts

Musical Thoughts & After-Thoughts

ALFRED BRENDEL

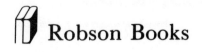 Robson Books

FIRST PUBLISHED IN GREAT BRITAIN IN 1976 BY
ROBSON BOOKS LTD., 28 POLAND STREET,
LONDON W1V 3DB. COPYRIGHT © 1976 ALFRED
BRENDEL

ISBN 0 903895 43 9

First impression September 1976
Second impression February 1977

Printed and bound by R. J. Acford Ltd.,
Chichester, Sussex.

ACKNOWLEDGEMENTS

The Preface, 'Schubert's Piano Sonatas, 1822-1828', Jeremy Siepmann's interview and 'The Process of Foreshortening in the First Movement of Beethoven's Sonata Op. 2, No. 1' were written in English. 'Form and Psychology in Beethoven's Piano Sonatas' and 'Liszt's Hungarian Rhapsodies' were translated from the German by Eugene Hartzell. All the other essays were translated by Paul Hamburger.

The lecture on 'Form and Psychology in Beethoven's Piano Sonatas' was first given in German at Professor Harald Kaufmann's Institut für musikalische Wertungsforschung in Graz in 1969, and in its English version at the 1970 Dartington Summer School. The lecture on 'Schubert's Piano Sonatas, 1822-1828' was first delivered at the Santa Fé Chamber Music Festival, 1973.

In a similar or considerably divergent form, the following articles have previously been printed:

'Notes on a Complete Recording of Beethoven's Piano Works' ('Anmerkungen zu einer Gesamtaufnahme der Klavierwerke Beethovens') – in *Hi Fi Stereophonie*, Karlsruhe, May 1966;

'Form and Psychology in Beethoven's Piano Sonatas' – in *Music and Musicians,* London, June 1971;

'Schubert's Piano Sonatas, 1822-1828' – as an accompaniment to a Philips boxed set containing my recordings of Schubert's later piano works, and, simultaneously, in *Hi Fi Stereophonie*, Karlsruhe, June 1975; it was also used as the basis for a BBC discussion with Stephen Plaistow in 1974;

'Liszt Misunderstood' ('Der missverstandene Liszt') – in *Phono,* Vienna 1961;

'Liszt's Hungarian Rhapsodies' – as a sleeve note for a Vanguard record, 1968;

'A Peculiar Serenity' ('Busoni, Vollender des Klavierspiels') – in *Österreichische Musikzeitschrift,* Vienna 1954;

'Arlecchino and Doktor Faust' – in *Die Presse,* Vienna, 2/3 April 1966;

'Remembering my Teacher' ('Edwin Fischer zum Gedenken') – in *Österreichische Musikzeitschrift,* Vienna 1960;

'Coping with Pianos' ('Vom Umgang mit Flügeln') – in *Hi Fi Stereophonie*, Karlsruhe, December 1974.

Jeremy Siepmann's interview originally appeared in *Music and Musicians,* London, December 1972; it is reprinted here in a slightly abridged version. Although its form is not that of an essay, I decided to include it because it makes a number of points which I thought fell within the scope of this book.

My thanks go to all the above publishers, as well as to Mr Lawrence Schoenberg, who kindly gave permission to quote from Arnold Schoenberg's notes on Busoni's *Entwurf einer neuen Ästhetik der Tonkunst.*

A.B.

CONTENTS

PREFACE

These writings on music, musicians and pianos do not represent the whole scope of my musical interests; they do not cover the ground of my entire repertory, nor do they show the proportion of my involvement with any composer. The occupation of a performer who tries to nurture a wide range of works leaves little room for the discipline of writing. Thus many plans have yet to be realized, accounts of my experiences with the Mozart concertos, Schoenberg's Piano Concerto Op. 42, and Liszt's B minor Sonata amongst them. A great deal of material on Beethoven's sonatas awaits inclusion in a more comprehensive study. And a dictionary of prejudice in music has been on my mind for a long while. Much of it will remain unwritten as long as I am able to put forward my arguments as a practising musician, by playing the piano.

Some of these articles are, at times, rather technical. It is impossible to avoid superficiality without, at certain points, talking about music in specialized terms. Some are only outlines for further investigation; I thus invite colleagues whose time is less limited than my own to test and pursue more thoroughly Beethoven's use of the technique of foreshortening which I have sketched in the lecture on 'Form and Psychology in Beethoven's Piano Sonatas'. To me it has explained a number of matters which other methods of analysis have left untouched. It makes a difference, of course, whether one verifies a method in one's mind, as I constantly do when I play, or listen to, Beethoven's works, or whether one tries to communicate its operation with the help of words. My use of the words 'psychology' and 'foreshortening' has been called in question. If anyone can think of more fitting terms, I shall be delighted to know them.

Those who look for contradictions will be amply satisfied. The profession of a performer is full of paradoxes, and he has to learn to live with them. He has to forget himself and control himself; he has to observe the composer's wishes to the letter and create the music on the spot; he has to be part of the music market and yet retain his integrity. While re-reading my older articles I found it necessary to revise them. While revising them, new essays emerged from my after-thoughts, either to clarify or to modify previous views. In the series of articles on Liszt, the first, adoring essay is put into perspective by other, more critical ones. None of my writings presumes to be the last word on anything.

I most gratefully acknowledge the help and valuable suggestions I have received from Paul Badura-Skoda (Vienna), Hermann Baron (London), Professor Gerald Fitzgerald (Melbourne), Hans Keller (London), Janet Rosenwald (Santa Fé, New Mexico), Professor René Taube (Washington D.C.), and Katharine Wilkinson (London), among many others. Finally, I should like to thank Jeremy Robson, who put the idea of a book to me – it would not have materialized without his gentle persistence – as well as my translators for their patience and perception, and Carolyn Fearnside, my editor at Robson Books, for the attention and care she has given to this book.

London, 1976   A.B.

BEETHOVEN

NOTES ON A COMPLETE RECORDING OF BEETHOVEN'S PIANO WORKS

I

I must begin with a qualification: this first recording of Beethoven's piano works, which I made for Vox-Turnabout between 1958 and 1964, is not entirely complete. There seemed to me little virtue in rescuing from oblivion works that are totally devoid of any touch of Beethoven's mastery and originality. It was without regret, therefore, that I omitted pieces like the deplorable Haibel Variations, which could have been written by any of Beethoven's contemporaries, as well as certain student exercises, *Albumblätter,* studies, sketches and curiosities, most of which were never intended for publication – pieces, that is, which are merely of interest to the historian. These include the total output of the Bonn period (among which are the Variations on a March by Dressler by the twelve-year-old Beethoven and the two preludes through all the major keys, curiously published later on as Op. 39), the Easy Sonata in C major, WoO 51, the Variations on the 'Menuet à la Vigano' by Haibel which I have already mentioned, the pieces WoO 52, 53, 55 (the Prelude in the style of Bach), 56, 61 and 61a, as well as the little dance movements WoO 81-86, of which I retained only the Six Écossaises, WoO 83, although in all likelihood these are transcriptions of an orchestral score, and the single extant copy, passed down by Nottebohm, may well be dubious in some of its detail. It is not for nothing that virtuosi have been stimulated again and again to make arrangements of these spirited pieces.

If I mention the fact that I concluded the series at the age of thirty-four, this is not to plead for mitigation, but to acquaint the reader with a circumstance that may explain certain features of these interpretations. Nothing was further from my mind than to suppose that I could present in my recordings anything like a definitive solution of the Beethoven problem. Nor was it my intention to supply the musical illustrations to any fashionable theory of Beethoven interpretation. I just plunged into an adventure, the consequences of which I could no more foresee than could the record company that had put its trust in me.

II

My work on the Beethoven series took five and a half years. One of the crosses the artist has to bear is that the date of a recording is so rarely indicated on the record sleeve. He is all too easily blamed or, almost worse, praised for interpretations that have lost some of their validity, at least as far as he himself is concerned. People expect an artist to develop, and yet they are only too ready to impale him, like an insect, on one of his renderings. The artist should have the right to identify his work with a certain phase of his development. It is only the continuous renewal of his vision – either in the form of evolution or of rediscovery – that can keep his music-making young.

The recordings of Beethoven's variation works, with the exception of the Diabelli Variations, were made in three stages between December 1958 and July 1960. There followed, at the turn of 1960/61, the last five sonatas, together with the Fantasy, Op. 77. In March 1962 I played the Sonatas Op. 31, Nos. 1 and 2, Op. 57 and Op. 90; in June and July of that year all the remaining sonatas between Op. 22 and Op. 81a. The early sonatas from Op. 2 to Op. 14 were recorded in December 1962 and January 1963. (By coincidence, I concluded my work on the thirty-two sonatas on my thirty-second birthday.) Finally, in July 1964, I played the miscellaneous pieces and the greatest of all piano works: the Diabelli Variations.

I recall a cold winter morning in a rather dilapidated Baroque mansion in Vienna; the logs in the fire-place of the hall where we recorded crackled so loudly that we had to throw them out of the window into the snow. Several changes in recording technique, and in the room and instrument, proved unavoidable. In the event, there were five groups of recordings: 1) the variation works, 2) the late sonatas, 3) the middle-period sonatas from Op. 22 on, 4) the early sonatas, 5) the miscellaneous pieces and the Diabelli Variations. The initiated will know that even the same concert grand does not stay the same over several months; that exactly the same microphone position – as if there were a jinx on it – does not always give the same results; that even technically satisfactory tapes may be distorted beyond recognition in the disc-pressing process. On some of the pressings of the late sonatas the dynamic range was reduced almost to uniformity; moreover, empty grooves of standard length were inserted between the movements, whether or not this suited the context or the composer's instructions, the reason given being that the customers liked it that way.

III

Beethoven's piano works pointed far into the future of piano building. Decades had to pass after his death before there were pianos – and pianists – equal to the demands of his *Hammerklavier* Sonata, Op. 106.

If one tries to play on Beethoven's Érard grand of 1803, which is kept in the instrument collection at the Vienna Kunsthistorische Museum, one thing becomes evident at once: its sound, dynamics and action have surprisingly little in common with the pianos of today. The tone of each single note has a distinct 'onset'; within its intimate confines, it is livelier and more flexible, and also more subject to change while it lasts. The difference in sound between bass, middle and top register is considerable (polyphonic playing!). The treble notes are short-lived and thin, and resist dynamic changes; the treble range is not conducive to cantilenas that want to rise above a gentle *piano.* Even in the clear and transparent, somewhat twangy bass register, the dynamic span is much narrower than on our instrument. One begins to see the reason for the permanent accompanying *piano* in the orchestral textures of Beethoven's piano concertos – even though, admittedly, the orchestral sound of his period cannot have been much like ours. If I had to compare the demands the Érard and the modern Steinway make on the physical power of the player, I would tend to think in terms of those made on a watchmaker and on a removal man!

A few years later, with the pianos of Streicher and Graf, a new, more rounded, more even and neutral sound came into being which, while dynamic scope continued to increase, became the norm throughout the nineteenth century. This sound is more closely related to the piano sound of today than to that of the older Hammerklavier, whose timbre was still derived from that of the harpsichord and clavichord. But by the time this new sound had become established, Beethoven had already composed a large portion of his piano works, and was afflicted by deafness.

We have to resign ourselves to the fact that whenever we hear Beethoven on a present-day instrument, we are listening to a sort of transcription. Anyone still having illusions about that will be disabused by a visit to a collection of old instruments. The modern concert grand, which I naturally used for my recordings, not only has the volume of tone demanded by modern orchestras, concert halls and ears; it also – and of this I am deeply convinced – does better justice to most of Beethoven's piano works than the Hammerklavier: its tone is far more colourful, orchestral, and rich in contrast, and these qualities do matter in Beethoven, as can be seen from his orchestral and chamber music. Some of the peculiarities of a Hammerklavier can only be approximated on a modern grand – for instance the sound of the *una corda* and even more the whisper of the *piano* stop. (In the studio, however, finesses of this kind did not always turn out as I wished, either because damping noises obliged me to change my style of playing, or because the technical specifications of the microphone did not permit me to go below a certain dynamic level.)

One must translate other characteristics of the Hammerklavier as best one can. The octave glissandi in the Prestissimo of the *Waldstein* Sonata, for example, were easier to execute on the older instrument: on the deep, heavy keys of a Steinway they can be brought off only by the use of brute force, which causes them to lose their scurrying *pianissimo* character. Very conscientious pianists, who cannot bear an untidy note, curb the tempo here and play wrist octaves. The only safe method of preserving the *pianissimo* character of this section without the help of a *piano* stop lies in imitating the sliding progress of the glissandi by distributing the passages between the hands, while reducing the bass octaves to their lower part.

IV

The variation works do not conform to the concept of Beethoven, the Olympian. Most of them are unknown even to pianists. Beside the sonatas, many of the variation works appear to be outpourings rather than structures. This is in the nature of the form, which derives from the improvisatory treatment of given material. The attraction (as well as the unevenness) of many variation works stems from the fact that something of the casualness and spontaneity of an improvisation survives in them. The charm of the moment, the lightness, mobility, sharp characterization, the humorous turn are here more important than organic growth. (Admittedly, this does not apply to the masterpieces of the genre: the Diabelli Variations, the Op. 34 and Op. 35 sets, and possibly the problematic C minor Variations.) In the witty, roguish finales we get a glimpse of Beethoven's art of improvisation, which otherwise only manifests itself – in a different, more passionate vein – in Op. 77, the Fantasy without basic tonality. Beethoven's at times rather peculiar sense of humour disports itself quite freely here – as for instance in the delightful 'Kind, willst du ruhig schlafen', my favourite piece in the lighter style, or in 'Venni amore'. In the 7th, 16th, 21st and 22nd variations of 'Venni amore', incidentally, there are distinct anticipations of Brahms, which make it quite obvious that the bearded successor of Beethoven must have known this work, and also 'Das Waldmädchen'. 'Quant'è più bello l'amor contadino' and 'Nel cor più non mi sento' (both after Paisiello) will give unalloyed pleasure to the innocent mind; also the Six Easy Variations on an original theme in G major. The Variations on 'Rule Britannia' are full of bizarre quirks. It is surprising that some of these works made their first appearance in the LP catalogue on this occasion.

What the pianist can learn, and the listener enjoy, in the variation works will be of advantage to both of them when they approach the sonatas. The variation works teach promptness of reaction, exactness and delicacy of characterization, and the ability to regard each variation as having its own separate identity. When compared to the suite, with its well-established formula of movements, the sonata too contained many new personal, private, characteristic elements which must have baffled the eighteenth-century listener. We also learn to be wary of over-dramatization in the sonatas, and begin to see the concept of the heroic Beethoven as a one-sided view representative of the bourgeois nineteenth century.

The miscellaneous piano pieces show us that Beethoven was also a master of the small form, though he rarely turned his attention to it. They are either loosely-gathered and small-scale collections, such as the Bagatelles Op. 33 and Op. 119 and the Écossaises; or they are held together by an inner unity, such as the 'trifles' of Op. 126 – lyrical, visionary, removed from the realm of the burlesque – with which Beethoven took his leave of the piano. By themselves stand the spirited, sparkling Polonaise, the hectic Fantasy, and the three Rondos: the two gracefully feminine ones of Op. 51, and the wild, masculine *alla zingara* work of his early Vienna days.

This last piece has an interesting history. It was published posthumously in 1828 under the title 'Die Wuth über den verlorenen Groschen ausgetobt in einer Kaprize' ('The Rage over the Lost Penny, Vented in a Caprice'); but only in 1832 was the so far unused opus number 129 affixed to it. In contrast to Czerny and Lenz, Hans von Bülow insisted with almost comical emphasis that this Rondo was a late-style work, repudiating any doubt on that point as 'worthy of the Kalmuck Oulibichev'.[1] The manuscript, discovered by Otto E. Albrecht in 1945, refutes Bülow's (and Riemann's) view: it also contains sketches for works dating from 1795-98. It can be deduced from the state of the manuscript that it served as the basis of the original edition, which was prepared by an unknown hand (Czerny? Schindler?), and certainly not by Beethoven himself. The title current today has been added to the manuscript in different handwriting. In Beethoven's own hand are the superscription 'Alla Ingharese quasi un Capriccio' and the designation 'Leichte Kaprize' on the fly-leaf. The manuscript bears all the marks of a sketchy first draft: uncompleted passages, particularly in the left-hand accompaniment, mistakes in part-writing, and a complete lack of dynamic markings and articulation signs. Unfortunately, it was only after my recording that I came across Erich Hertzmann's thorough investigation of the autograph in the *Musical Quarterly*, XXXII, 1946, as well as the manuscript itself, so that not all the mistakes of the original edition have been expunged from my performance. An exact text of the piece can be found in the edition I prepared for the *Wiener Urtext* series.

The beautiful 'Andante favori' and the C minor Allegretto are remnants of Beethoven's work on the Sonatas Op. 53 and Op. 10,

---

[1] *Translator's note:* Alexander Oulibichev (1795-1858), an early Russian biographer of Beethoven.

No. 1, respectively. The wonderful, well-known 'Für Elise' (or Therese) and another, later *Albumblatt* in B flat major, a memento to Marie Szymanowska, can hold their own with the best of the Bagatelles, while the Op. 119 and Op. 126 sets look ahead to the Romantic cycles of Schumann, from *Papillons* to *Kreisleriana*.

V

The study of a composer's works appears to me a more profitable pursuit than any pilgrimage to tombs and shrines, or, for that matter, the perusal of a large quantity of critical writing about him. A great deal has been written about Beethoven's sonatas, most of it of negligible value. (On the other hand, despite Tovey's outstanding attempt, I do not yet know of any exhaustive analysis of the Diabelli Variations.) Generally, all one can expect is a little amusement, albeit at the author's expense: thus, a Beethoven biographer from the beginning of this century tells us that the *Waldstein* Sonata 'had at some time acquired the nickname "Horror", presumably because of the thrusting, agitated figuration and the surprising modulations of its opening which are apt to make one shudder.' The author's shudderings are based on a misunderstanding: the *Waldstein* Sonata is known in France as 'L'Aurore'.

Among the older Beethoven literature, the commentaries of Czerny, *Über den richtigen Vortrag der sämtlichen Beethoven'schen Klavierwerke* ('On the proper performance of all Beethoven's works for the piano'), newly edited by Paul Badura-Skoda, are well worth reading; of slightly lesser importance are the writings of Schindler, Ries and Lenz. The interest of Prod'homme's book *The Piano Sonatas of Beethoven* lies in its inclusion of Beethoven's sketches.

Czerny, taking the Cello Sonata, Op. 69, as an example, describes the repeated striking of two notes connected by a tie, an effect later known as *Bebung,* which is surely also intended in the Adagio of Op. 106 and in the recitative of Op. 110. The information he gives on the later works is scanty. Yet he does make this comment on the variations of Op. 109: 'The whole movement in the style of Handel and Seb. Bach' – a remark which startled me only for a moment. It is rather amusing to see how indignant the self-important and unreliable Schindler, Beethoven's first biographer, waxes about Czerny's clumsy, but generally sensible and honest, commentaries. Anyone nowadays venturing to play the first movement of Op. 10, No. 1 in the manner recommended by Schindler would cause some shaking of heads. His suggestion to add two crotchet rests between each phrase in bars 16-21 makes the passage sound rhetorically overblown, while his addition of two fermatas in bar 93 and a cæsura before the *fp* in bar 94 I find downright silly.

Among the more recent books on the sonatas, that of my teacher Edwin Fischer is outstanding; while containing only a fraction of what Fischer had to say about these works, the loving care with which his often quite unobtrusive advice is given makes it more useful than many more exhaustive investigations. Bülow's and Schnabel's editions of the sonatas may, on account of their copious footnotes, jokingly be counted among the Beethoven literature. Both deserve respect as manifestations of strong personalities, and are highly stimulating owing to the temperaments of their authors. Both frequently invite disagreement. Bülow is the first editor to be credited with the attempt to retrace mentally Beethoven's compositional processes; unfortunately, his intellectual method was not equal to his purpose, and he did not pay sufficient attention to the original material. Schnabel, whom I respect as one of the great pianists of his time, was in many ways anti-Bülow: he removed the latter's autocratic 'corrections', but accepted a number of obvious mistakes in the original texts with a kind of pedantic deference. In his choice of readings, I find Schenker generally more convincing than Schnabel, who is said to have been not too happy about his edition in later years. Both Bülow and Schnabel invented highly original fingerings, as did d'Albert, who had a fondness for playing bass notes with the thumb; in his comments, however, he was more sparing of words than his colleagues. At the well-known disputed passage in the *Hammerklavier* Sonata, before the entry of the first movement's recapitulation, he just says 'A sharp, of course'. As a matter of fact, I play A natural.

Of all the analyses, those by Tovey, Schenker and Ratz (Op. 106) proved more helpful to me than Riemann or Nagel.[1]

---

[1]Since this article was written, at least three new books merit attention: Jürgen Uhde's *Beethovens Klaviermusik* (Reclam, 3 volumes), Rudolph Réti's *Thematic Patterns in Sonatas of Beethoven* (Faber & Faber), and Charles Rosen's *The Classical Style* (Faber & Faber).

VI

For a player to study autographs and first prints is more than a hobby; in spite of modern *Urtext* editions, it is frequently a necessity. When does an *Urtext* edition deserve to be so called? When, basing itself on all existing original sources, it reproduces the text as the composer might have wished to see it, while at the same time discussing mistakes, omissions and doubtful passages in detailed critical notes, quoting all divergent readings, and substantiating editorial decisions. Heinrich Schenker's exemplary edition of the sonatas and the widely esteemed Henle edition come closest to these requirements, without entirely fulfilling them; the edition by Craxton and Tovey regrettably ignores many of Beethoven's articulation markings, while giving phrasing indications of dubious value. The definitive editorial work is still to be done.

Using the early prints as the point of reference, I myself corrected a large part of the variation works, since at the time of recording no tolerably reliable edition of the second volume was yet in existence. In connection with the recording of the miscellaneous pieces (Bagatelles, Rondos, etc.) I began to prepare an *Urtext* edition of all those pieces I was including in my gramophone series. Certain important documents, however, did not come to my notice until after the recording sessions were over – as for instance the autograph of the 'Easy Caprice' and the London first editions of some works, the significance of which was not realized until Alan Tyson's book *The Authentic English Editions of Beethoven* (Faber & Faber) was published in 1963.

Let me give one or two examples:

The London first edition (The Royal Harmonic Institution) of the Sonata Op. 106 has in bar 116 of the Adagio as first semiquaver in the right hand an F sharp^3, in contrast to the usual D sharp^3 of the Vienna first edition (Artaria) and all later editions known to me.

This F sharp[3] not only strikes me as stronger and nobler, it also fits better into the melodic line of the second subject: the three-note motive (rising third, falling second) determines its structure up to bar 120.

In other cases I mistakenly relied on the well-known *Urtext* editions, as the following will illustrate:

The six-times repeated F_1 of the pedal point in bars 373-78 of the Fugue in Op. 106 was tacitly provided with ties by Schenker, but these belong only to the overlying trill on B flat$_1$. The logical argument in favour of re-striking these notes is furnished by bars 379-80: the sixfold F_1 reappears here, this time in rhythmic diminution.

In the Polonaise, Op. 89, we find the following sequence (bars 19-21, also 64-66):

The Henle edition altered, without comment, the bass of the third crotchet of bars 19 and 64 into B flat,[1] thus depriving this *pianissimo* passage of its special harmonic piquancy. Both these examples are in contradiction to the sources.

I have since changed my mind about the execution of certain details, so that today, in the ninth variation of the *Eroica* Variations, Op. 35, I would play the acciaccaturas in bars 13-17 not before, but together with the left hand. In some cases my reading was inaccurate, or my fancy permitted itself an indefensible variant, as in Op. 28, second movement, bars 72-73. I apologize!

VII

Every generation of musicians is unconsciously influenced by the editions with which it has grown up. My own generation, at least in Central Europe, became accustomed to using editions which respect the text of the composer. Yet necessary though it is to reject the accretions foisted upon the music by the older editors, the restored text is all too easily invested by its users with an autonomous signifi-

[1] In recent reprints the error has been corrected.

cance which it does not merit. All of us are apt to forget at times that musical notes can only suggest, that expression marks can only supplement and confirm what we must, first and foremost, read from the face of the composition itself.

I should therefore like to propose that the words *Werktreue* and *Texttreue*[1] be banished from the vocabulary. They have become the feather bed of the academic Classicists. The 'fidelity' referred to here smacks overmuch of 'trust': blind trust, that is, in the self-sufficiency of the letter; trust in the notion that the work will speak for itself as long as the interpreter does not interpose his personality. Let there be no misunderstanding: it is far from my intention to set myself up as the advocate of self-indulgence. The virtuoso who unhesitatingly adapted the music of the past to his own style of playing and composing belongs to a bygone age. Gone are the days when the 'edition', the revision made by a famous virtuoso or teacher, was more important than the original text. That state of affairs, commonly associated with the successors of Liszt, dates back, incidentally, to much earlier times. Carl Czerny – the teacher of Liszt and pupil of Beethoven – did not have any scruples about publishing with Diabelli under his own name a *Grand Duo brillant à quatre mains,* with the minutely engraved subtitle 'arrangé d'après la Sonate de L. van Beethoven, Oeuv. 47'. This is nothing other than a piano duet arrangement of the *Kreutzer* Sonata! (See plate facing p. 60.)

The Romantic era did not yet know a historically-minded style of interpretation. People played everything 'the way they felt', their minds scarcely accessible to arguments of historical propriety. (Editors like Bischoff and Kullak, who aimed at meticulously cleaning the musical text of additions, remained outsiders.) This attitude appeared natural and legitimate until the time when tonality began to disintegrate. In other words, when one could no longer compose or improvise 'modern' cadenzas for Classical piano concertos, the practice of interpreting Classical works in a 'modern' manner also became obsolete. The innocent self-assurance of the virtuoso was gone – a revolutionary development indeed. In its wake there evolved the editing techniques of the *Urtext* publication. The investigation of

[1] *Translator's note: Werktreue,* commonly used in German musicology, signifies the performer's fidelity to the intentions of the composer, *Texttreue* his fidelity to the text of a work. Since no simple English translation offers itself, I have decided to use the German terms in the context of this essay as well as in the title of its supplement, in the hope that – *pace* the author's distrust if not of the words, then of their implications! – they will be accepted by the English music lover with the kindness he has bestowed on the word *Urtext.*

the performing traditions of past ages produced, apart from some misconceptions, a number of genuine insights, which affected the style of Mozart interpretation in particular. The first era of 'historicism' in the short history of public concert-giving had dawned. Its repercussions on the Late Romantic age itself both fascinated and inhibited more than one generation of performers. The loss of self-confidence was often followed by a rigid faith in the letter. People began to play every sort of appoggiatura on the beat, and string quartets would play all four parts equally loudly just because Beethoven had marked them all with the same *forte* or *piano*. The harshness thus created was considered Classical by many, and still is today in some circles. The dogma according to which every whim of the composer, however unreasonable, must be accepted with reverence, absolved performers from the effort of thinking for themselves. No engraver's error in a first print, no slip of the pen in an autograph was so absurd that it could not be hailed as a bold stroke of genius.

During the same period, the gramophone record established itself. At first a convenient means of preserving the fleeting, unrepeatable impression of a performance, the record, and with it the recording artist, soon laid claim to greater things: all elements of improvisation must stand back in favour of an ideal performance, a definitive rendering divested of any fortuitous aspects. The taking of risks – for which one needs self-confidence – lost its attraction and relevance. The image of the machine in its impassive efficiency gained power over many minds; it became an obsession to strive for perfection. In mistrusting their own nature, artists denied themselves access to the nature of music. The usual symptoms of this are that emotions become either completely dried up or wilfully superimposed. Often, both extremes are to be found in the same person; the vital area between them remains largely unfrequented.

We artists of today have to bear the burden of this paternal heritage, and we feel drawn towards the great ones among our grandfathers. Most younger musicians of all countries, for instance, will readily agree in their admiration for the conductor Furtwängler.

VIII

What, then, should the interpreter do? Two things, I believe. He should try to understand the intentions of the composer, and he should seek to give each work the strongest possible effect. Often, but not always, the one will result from the other.

To understand the composer's intentions means to translate them into one's own understanding. Music cannot 'speak for itself'. The notion that an interpreter can simply switch off his personal feelings and instead receive those of the composer 'from above', as it were, belongs to the realm of fable. What the composer actually meant when he put pen to paper can only be unravelled with the help of one's own engaged emotions, one's own senses, one's own intellect, one's own refined ears. Such an attitude is as far removed from sterile 'fidelity' as it is from transcription-mania. To force or to shun the 'personal approach' is equally questionable; where this does not come of itself, any effort is in vain.

The second requirement, that of giving the music the strongest possible effect, can be seen as an attack on the same problem ('What is appropriate to the music?') from a different angle. But let no one imagine that the greatest possible effect can be equated with the noisiest – or, for that matter, the least noisy – public acclaim. The crucial distinction is not between, on the one hand, that incessant, extrovert high tension so beloved of naïve listeners, and, on the other, the kind of music-making that fancies itself in the garb of a penitential hair shirt. Those performances that are historically 'most correct' are not always the ones that leave us with the most cherished memories. It would be wrong to modify such memories after the event on Christian Morgenstern's humorous principle that 'what may not be, cannot be'. It is our moral duty to make music in as visionary, moving, mysterious, thoughtful, amusing, graceful a manner as we are able to; but this raises the question 'What is it that will move, shatter, edify or amuse our contemporaries?' There results the paradox that a consummate musical interpretation in which time and occasion seem to have been transcended, in which the shackles of historicism appear to have been broken and thrown off, can only be achieved in concord with our own age. The musical master-work is a power-house of multiple energies. To release those that will strike the noblest, the most elemental resonance in modern man – it is this task that raises the *Urtext* interpreter above the status of museum curator. A task, also, that should restore to him some of his lost self-respect.

(1966)

WERKTREUE – AN AFTERTHOUGHT

I

On account of my essay on Beethoven's piano works, I have been branded an opponent of *Werktreue,* while the actual arguments I brought against this by now rather antiquated word were conveniently forgotten. My strictures were directed against the formation of the word and the pedantic aura surrounding it, not against its real meaning, which, however, is rarely intended. In any case, the proper meaning of *Werktreue* is at best marginal and suggestive; *Texttreue,* by comparison, is rather more concrete. As my essay shows, my reasons for disliking this word do not lie in any supposed hatred of a father-figure, in any attitude of protest against the authority of the composer, which would indeed ill befit a musical interpreter. But equally, I have never considered myself to be merely the passive recipient of the composer's commands, preferring to promote his cause of my own free will and in my own way.

I have been made immune to blind faith by the years I spent under the Nazi régime. In the slave mentality of that era, not only words like 'faith' and 'fatherland', but also the word 'fidelity' suffered shameful abuse. Even a fairly harmless word like 'work', when used in conjunction with 'fidelity', strikes a militant pose; for me, after all these years, the term *Werktreue* still smacks of credulous, parade-ground solemnity.

The Vienna of the post-war years – a further background to my aversion – presented a mixed picture, musically speaking. Furtwängler and Clemens Krauss, each in his own way, set their seal on the Philharmonic Concerts and on the wonderful sound of the orchestra. The Nicolai Concerts of Furtwängler, in which Beethoven's Ninth was regularly played, were high points in my musical calendar; but so were the New Year Concerts of Krauss with their inimitable, ironically detached performances of the waltzes and polkas of the Strauss family. In the Vienna State Opera company were a number of young female singers whose looks rivalled the splendour of their voices. Mozart's operas, though still lacking the appoggiaturas abolished by Gustav Mahler, were performed with a freshness and an enthusiasm hardly equalled since.

The teaching of music in Vienna, on the other hand, was dominated by a strict Classicism. Having recently come across Busoni's writings, I admired his aesthetics, which ran counter to the Viennese literal-mindedness, and was impressed by the aristocratic reserve of his reply to the polemical attack in Pfitzner's pamphlet *Futuristengefahr* ('The Futurist Danger'). After recording Busoni's *Fantasia Contrappuntistica* for a small, now defunct gramophone company, I played it again in 1954 before a sparse Viennese audience. Busoni's concept of a 'Young Classicism' had no more to do with the academic Classicism prevalent in Vienna than with the sort of 'new music' which was performed there in those days. It was quite a time before twentieth-century music began to recover from the dislocation of 1938, and the gap was temporarily filled by works of a neo-Classical or neo-Baroque stamp. Piano students played Beethoven as if he had learnt composition from Hindemith. Romanticism was disparaged as something vague, disorderly, dreamy, Utopian; something that might be right for the Philharmonic Concert audiences, but not for people with more progressive tastes. It was identified with pathos, sentimentality, luxuriance, frequent arpeggio chords and the neglect of strict time-keeping. Modernity was equated with anti-Romanticism. There seemed to be no place for illusions in the stark reality of those years. What went unnoticed was that Classicism itself was one of the illusions of the moment. Despite an occasional undercurrent of aggressiveness, and despite its apparent reluctance to take itself seriously, Classicism simulated an order which no longer existed.

Since then, the meagre frame of music has acquired more body. Schubert's sonatas and Mahler's symphonies have experienced a nostalgic revival. 'Austere' is no longer the highest epithet that can be bestowed upon a musical rendering. Radio stations no longer suppress resonance; the spatial nature of sound has re-established itself.

Musicians show their colours once again. They are tired of calcula-
tion, and give a chance to chance.

Parallel to this development, a change has overtaken the
interpretation of the music of the past. There is no danger now that a
new generation of pianists will 'invest the text with an autonomous
significance which it does not merit'. Indeed, the prevailing ambition
to do better than just reel off the notes piously and phlegmatically
reminds one at times of those conductors of the old school who con-
cealed their lack of textual learning behind the assertion that 'all
music is at best an arrangement'. Perhaps in the age of aleatory music
a reminder that the observance of the notated text is obligatory would
not come amiss.

II

To read music correctly does not only mean to perceive what is
written down (although this in itself is far more difficult than is commonly assumed), but also to *understand* the musical symbols. Though
the correct perception of these symbols is only a starting point, the
attention given to it is of decisive importance to the process that follows: a faulty foundation endangers the stability of the whole edifice.
To go to the original sources rather than take the various editors on
trust, to find out which are the proper sources to consult, then to look
these up in libraries or obtain photocopies of them – all this is not a
waste of time, nor does it distract from the essentials. Even Bülow
would not have persisted in his arguments against the repeat in the
finale of the *Appassionata* if the autograph of this work had been
known to him, for in it the word *repetizione* is written out in fearsome,
commanding letters.

Beethoven's autographs are often difficult to read, but it would be
wrong to conclude from this that his notation, let alone his
composition, was imprecise. The chaotic side of Beethoven's nature,
so startlingly apparent from the scrawl of his handwriting, is brought
to order in the finished compositions. The effort it cost him to achieve
that order gives it its particular stability. However, Beethoven's
untiring labour over details hardly ever interferes with his conception
of the whole. On the contrary: in some of the early works the detail is
not always worthy of the grand design; in some of the middle-period
works the detail is at times lost in the wide expanse of the whole,

receding into the background as if viewed through the wrong end of a telescope; and in some of the works between the *Appassionata* and the late sonatas the notation is surprisingly careless on occasion, as in the left-hand line of the second movement of the Sonata in F sharp, Op. 78. But these are only exceptions which prove the rule – that Beethoven's self-discipline exerted its strict control even when he was taking the most adventurous risks.

The text of the *Hammerklavier* Sonata, the autograph of which is lost, is a special case, and it poses a whole series of problems. On the one hand, the structure of this gigantic work appears to be a triumph of logic without equal; and yet, on the other, there is Beethoven's letter to his former pupil Ries, who was then living in London, in which he gives him permission to destroy this structure: he may transpose, if he wishes, the order of the two middle movements (the London first edition does in fact have the Adagio before the Scherzo), and he may, 'if necessary', omit the introduction to the Fugue. Beside such a proposition, Busoni's idea of putting the Adagio and Fugue into a programme without the first two movements appears positively innocuous. Beethoven's letter cannot be explained away as an act of negligence. Could it be that in this rare instance chaos predominated, turning the creator against his own creation?[1] The metronome marks have an equally detrimental effect: with one exception, they are all hurried, not to say maniacally overdriven. In the first movement particularly, the prescribed tempo cannot be attained, or even approached, on any instrument in the world, by any player at all, be he the devil incarnate!

My recommendation to young pianists is to put their reading ability to the test by means of Bartók's Suite Op. 14 and Berg's Sonata Op. 1. (The aid of a tape recorder is indispensable.) Compared with the subtly differentiated symbols which Bartók and Berg use to convey their intentions, Beethoven's notation is still sketchy: a new technique of notation was in the making. It is therefore all the more important to observe every sign written down by Beethoven. His ability to notate the essential without overloading the text with

[1]Beethoven's severing of his greatest fugue from the Quartet in B flat, Op. 130, is another case of apparent self-destruction. The 'Grosse Fuge' was composed as its finale and without any doubt belongs there. Beethoven substituted a comparatively lightweight rondo, which is now usually played, and agreed that the 'Grosse Fuge' would be published separately, in its string version as Op. 133, and in a piano four-hand version of his own as Op. 134. Beethoven's consent may have had commercial reasons: he needed money, and the publisher offered him separate fees for each version of the fugue.

instructions has been equalled by very few later composers, and bettered by none. To a greater extent than in the piano works of Mozart, Beethoven's expression marks are founded in the logic of the composition.[1] Among the most important gifts a Beethoven player can have is the power to visualize, in an almost geographical sense, the entire panorama of varying dynamic levels embodied in a work – like looking at a landscape and taking in at a single glance its valleys and mountain-tops.

Beethoven's notation is more modern than that of his contemporaries, with the possible exception of Weber. One can take it more literally than Mozart's, in whose piano music every degree of marking is to be found, ranging from the excessive to the non-existent, and in which, moreover, symbols taken from the sphere of the string player (bowings) and the singer (accents, dynamics) have to be translated into their pianistic equivalents. In his notation Beethoven rejected a number of Baroque conventions. Schubert, and even Chopin and Schumann, occasionally notate divided triplets as dotted rhythms, but there are not many instances in Beethoven's piano music, after the stormy second subject in the Rondo of the Sonata Op. 2, No. 2, where dotted rhythms have to be adapted to triplets. In his commentaries on Beethoven's piano works, Czerny points out that in the Adagio of the *Moonlight* Sonata the semiquaver of the melody should always fall *after* the accompanying triplet note, a remark which shows how foreign such a procedure still was to contemporary practice. In Beethoven's use of the turn, the Baroque manner of execution has survived in one or two cases, whereby the rhythm of figure *a* is played as in figure *b:*

This applies in pieces of moderate tempo and graceful or coquettish character. (A slur over group *a* would be a counter-indication, for then the semiquaver would have to retain its full length.)

[1]This does not mean that there are no mistakes, misjudgements, vagaries or ambiguities in Beethoven. Misjudgements of balance are familiar to anyone who has had practical experience of his piano concertos. The *piano* entry of the soloist in the development of the first movement of the G major Concerto (bar 192) was, as Nottebohm has already observed, later changed by Beethoven into a *forte* – much to the benefit of clarity. And in the London first edition of the Sonata Op. 31, No. 3, it is interesting to see that the main subject of the finale is marked *forte*, whereas the Vienna first edition, published at about the same time, has *piano*.

III

Among Beethoven's expression marks, there are some whose particular significance I should like to investigate.

1) Beethoven's accentuation signs: *sforzando, fortepiano, rinforzando*

What is a musical accent? Is it a sudden dynamic impact, fading into a *diminuendo,* as visually suggested by the $>$ sign? The pianist, whose instrument has acquired the reputation of a percussion instrument, should be particularly wary of automatically interpreting it this way. Yet it is above all the *sforzandi* of Beethoven that receive the most unthinking treatment: on all instruments, it has become habitual to 'stab' at them.

What, then, is an accent? A note (or chord) the intensity of which must be underlined. This can be done in various ways. An *sf* may swell out a note; it may plummet into it; it may have a *cantabile* character – on orchestral instruments, an increase in vibrato may be sufficient to lift out an *sf* note from its neighbours. With many of Beethoven's *sforzandi,* a note will retain its intensity over its whole duration, or over the greater part of it. Accompanying voices, moving in shorter note values, will often support the intensity of the longer note.[1] Here we have a clear case for breaking the general rule that one *sf* applies only to one single note. (In Mozart, it is not unusual for the effect of an *sf* to extend over several notes, until the next *piano.*[2])

What is the pianist to do, since in theory he cannot influence the sound of a note once it is struck? In the first place, he must rid himself completely of the prejudice that to do so is impossible. Singing, as an idea and a reality, must become second nature to him to the extent that even the recalcitrant piano will be at his service. The sound of sustained notes on the piano can be modified *a*) with the help of accompanying voices, if there are any; *b*) with the help of syncopated pedalling; *c*) with the help of certain movements which make the pianist's conception of *cantabile* actually visible to the audience. Such movements will strongly affect not only the onset of the note,

[1] Piano Concerto Op. 15, first movement, bar 97; third movement, bars 28-32.
 Piano Concerto Op. 19, second movement, bars 31-34.
[2] K 595, first movement, bars 54, 57, etc.   K 331, first movement, variation 1.
 K 456, second movement, variation 1.

but also its preparation and continuation. But there are some *crescendi* on a single note which only the suggestive power of the artist in the concert hall will convey.

Let me now discuss the individual accentuation signs.

There is no general rule determining the quality and quantity of a *sforzando*. It is governed by its musical significance, which has to be discovered by the player in each instance. In a lyrical context, it will rarely be violent. If it occurs in an *ff* passage, the player will have to husband his strength in order to make the accent stand out above the general level of tone. Not every *sf* is unprepared. It is possible for an *sf* to give added radiance to the climax of a rounded phrase, or to lend some of its weight to the preceding note or group of notes. When he means an *sf* to decrease gradually, Beethoven gives it a *diminuendo* pin.

The *fortepiano* must be taken at its face value: as a *forte* which is followed by a *piano* as quickly as possible. The same principle applies to the signs *mfp, ffp* and *fpp*. In the orchestra, *fp* means that the *piano* should occur within the note so marked, unless that is very short; it is, then, a vehement accent with its centre of gravity at the start of the note. On Beethoven's Hammerklaviers with their rapidly fading tone, a *fortepiano* chord like the one at the beginning of the *Sonate Pathétique* still had an orchestral quality. The sound, as Schindler reminds us, should have died away almost completely before one plays on. (Edwin Fischer and Eduard Erdmann attempted, with varying success, to produce orchestral *fp* effects on the modern grand by tricks of pedalling.) In general, however, *fp* in piano music will mean that it is the succeeding note that has to be played softly. By comparison, Schubert's *fp* direction is much less absolute: it often trails away in a spacious *decrescendo*. Beethoven's *fp*, besides denoting an abrupt accent, may stand for something else: it may mark out the last note of a longish *forte* passage which is to be succeeded by a sudden *piano*. In contrapuntal piano writing, the *fp* may also serve to underline and sustain the note of longest value while the other parts fall back at once to *piano*. This is the opposite of the sustained *sf* note which, as I have said, receives the support of the accompanying parts.

In the sign *sfp*, the *sf* has relative, the *p* absolute meaning.

The *rinforzando* is used by Beethoven in two ways:

i) as a *cantabile* emphasis on one or several notes, usually in a lyrical context (it does not by any means always extend over several notes, as is shown by the *rinforzandi* in the slow movements of the Sonatas Op. 7, Op. 10, No. 2, and Op. 10, No. 3);

ii) in his later works, as a signal that *all* the notes up to the next dynamic sign should be played with greater insistence, usually in preparation for the dynamic climax to be reached during a *crescendo.* Instead of the climactic moment, however, there may be a surprising *subito piano,* as in the second movement of Op. 109.

The word *sforzato* is used by Beethoven only in the first movement of the *Emperor* Concerto. There, it asks for the player's energetic attention to all the notes of an extended section, the figuration of which he should not mistake for a neutral background. On the contrary, these passages are meant to put up active resistance to the leading, or opposing, voice. It goes without saying that in bar 136 ff. this resistance will have to be confined within narrow dynamic limits if the bassoon is to remain audible.

In Beethoven's notation, the accentuation mark in most common use since the nineteenth century – > – indicates slight accents that do not achieve the intensity of an *sf.*

2) *pianissimo* and *dolce*

Whereas the dynamic degrees between *p* and *ff* can serve a wide range of expressive purposes, according to the character of the passage, Beethoven's *pianissimo* is what Rudolf Kolisch called a 'pianissimo misterioso'. We enter into a sphere distinctly removed from *piano,* a sphere of awe and wonder. His *dolce,* too, has its own emotional climate: my translation is 'tenderly committed'. *Dolce* tells the player: 'Identify yourself with this phrase; do not control it from outside.' It begs for loving attention and flinches from mechanical coldness.

3) *espressivo*

I should like to refer to three *espressivo* markings in Beethoven's late sonatas. In the first movement of Op. 101 we find *espressivo semplice.* In the last movement, there is a *dolce poco espressivo,* and in the second movement of Op. 109, a *poco espressivo* occurs twice, followed a few bars later by an *a tempo.* What do these directions tell us? In the first place, it is highly illuminating to discover that *espressivo* and *semplice* are not mutually exclusive, as the general manner of *espressivo* playing might lead one to believe. Secondly, we learn that *dolce* and *espressivo* emit different emotional signals. The heartfelt gentleness of *dolce* generally keeps away from minor keys. *Dolce* is soothing, or conveys tender rapture. However luminous it may be, it shines with an inner light, whereas *espressivo* distinctly addresses the outer world. Where the two appear together (as *dolce poco espressivo* in Op. 101, or as *cantabile dolce ed espressivo* in the first movement of Op. 106), the *dolce* is to be given additional weight. For that is what *espressivo* demands: a perceptible increase in emotional emphasis over the foregoing passage. The philological justification for drawing out the tempo a little under the pressure of this emphasis is provided by the tempo indications of Op. 109.

4) Pedal

Beethoven writes pedal marks:

i) perhaps most frequently when pedal points are to be held in the bass, as in the Rondo of the *Waldstein* Sonata;

ii) in a delicately veiled atmosphere (Czerny speaks of an 'Aeolian harp'): for example in the Largo of the C minor Concerto, and in the recitative in the first movement of the Sonata Op. 31, No. 2;

iii) when all the notes of a chord or arpeggio are to be sustained, but this cannot be done by the hands alone;

iv) when the pedal is to be used in a way unexpected by the player, as in the hammered chords in the Presto of Op. 27, No. 2, or the diminished-seventh chords in the third movement of Op. 101;

v) when the duration of the pedal sound is to be precisely defined against surrounding rests: for example in the two arpeggio chords before the epilogue in the slow movement of the G major Concerto, where a subdivision into semiquaver rests occurs.

It can be seen that Beethoven notates the pedal only when he wishes to obviate misunderstandings, or when aiming at unusual effects.

5) *ritardando*

Czerny's *School of Piano-Playing,* Op. 500, (1842), enumerates the circumstances in which a slowing of the tempo may suggest itself, even though none is notated by the composer. According to Czerny, 'A *ritardando* may be made to advantage *a)* in passages which form a return to the main subject;

b) on notes which lead up to a single small part of a *cantabile* line [?];

c) on sustained notes that are to be struck with particular emphasis, and which are followed by shorter notes;

d) during the transition to a new tempo, or to a movement wholly different from the preceding one;

e) immediately before a fermata;

f) when a very lively passage, or some brilliant figure-work, gives way to a *diminuendo* introducing a soft, delicate run;

g) on ornaments consisting of a large number of quick notes which cannot be squeezed [!] into the correct tempo;

h) occasionally in heavily marked passages, where a strong *crescendo* leads to a new movement or to the end of the piece;

i) in very whimsical, capricious or fanciful movements, in order to highlight their character better;

k) finally, in almost every case where the composer has put *espressivo;* and

l) at the end of every long trill forming a halt and a cadence in *diminuendo,* as well as on gentle cadences in general.

(NB: It is understood that the word *ritardando* as used above includes all other terms which indicate a greater or lesser slowing of the tempo.)'

These observations of Czerny's, as well as the musical meaning of various passages marked *ritardando,* make it clear that up to the middle of the nineteenth century no distinction was made between *ritardando* and *ritenuto.* A *ritardando* (or *rallentando*) mark may therefore tell us either to *become* gradually slower, or to *be* slower at once. An awareness of this will make it much easier for us to perform convincingly the *rallentando* passages in the first movement of Op. 2, No. 2.

IV

The same Czerny who regards tempo modifications as a prerequisite of beautiful playing tells us apropos of Beethoven's First Piano Concerto:

'In fast passages, the player must not forget that some orchestral instruments usually play along with him, either by way of

furnishing an accompaniment or in the execution of a melody. In such passages, therefore, he must restrain his humour more fully than in the rendering of a solo piece, and at rehearsal everything that may be necessary in this respect must be diligently dealt with.'
('Humour' in the language of the time means 'whim' or 'caprice'.)

Another remark of Czerny's illuminates the performing conventions at the beginning of the last century even more:

'In Beethoven's last concerto works it is expedient for the director of the orchestra to conduct from his own copy of the clavier part, since the correct rendering of these works cannot be divined [!] from the violin part.'

The scores of concertos were frequently published many years after the solo and orchestral parts, if they were published at all. The practice of conducting concertos from the first violin part had survived into our century, as I learnt during my student days in the late forties. The teacher of the conducting class at the Graz Conservatory set me the laborious task of reconstructing the score of the First Violin Concerto by Spohr from the orchestral parts. When the elderly librarian, himself a retired Kapellmeister, handed me the orchestral material, he just shook his head and said, 'What do you need a full score for? In my day we conducted this sort of thing from the violin part!' What would our hypersensitive ears make of a performance, mounted after a single rehearsal, of a work whose meaning had to be 'divined' by the musicians, none of whom knew the score? How anxiously everyone must have kept time to avoid utter confusion!

Like most great writers for the piano, Beethoven was in no lesser degree a composer of ensemble music. The soloist should therefore never completely lose contact with the performing style of the orchestra or string quartet, unless he happens to concentrate on those composers who wrote exclusively for the piano, as is the case with Chopin, the young Schumann and the young Liszt.

My relations with the metronome are on the cool side, and I resent it if the classics are subjected to the rhythmic discipline of a jazz musician. The great conductors, who allow an orchestra to breathe, should be our model; their tempo modifications will often differ from those of the average soloist. Liberties in tempo of a 'humorous' kind, which a good orchestra would not play nor a good conductor conduct, are usually out of place in the performing of Beethoven's sonatas as well. Despite his self-sufficiency, the pianist will be able to claim exemption from the rules of ensemble playing only where the symphonic framework of a sonata is broken up by recitatives or improvisatory passages, where particular eloquence is desired (as in the fifth Bagatelle of Op. 33, marked *con una certa espressione parlante*), and in those capricious finales which Beethoven, according to Czerny, 'played humorously'.

Whilst I readily believe the reports of Beethoven's contemporaries that, at least in his early years, his piano-playing 'mostly stayed strictly in time', surely that kind of time-keeping has nothing in common with the metronomic awareness one acquires through aquaintance with jazz and Stravinsky.

If someone intends to play something with the utmost simplicity, he will in the first place try to achieve this by an absolute evenness of tone and rhythm. It may be years before he realizes that his vision of the desired effect has, paradoxically, closed his eyes to the best way of achieving it. The projection of simplicity can be a very complex business. An exceptional reservoir of nuances – even though they may remain unused – and a considerable degree of sensitivity and inner freedom are required if the result is not to be, instead of simplicity, emptiness and boredom. Similarly, on the subject of musical time, a 'psychological' tempo is to be distinguished from the metronomic one: an interpreter who follows the flow of the music as naturally as possible – and by 'natural' I refer of course here to the nature of the music, not to that of the player – will always give the 'psychological' listener the impression that he is 'staying in tempo'.

Those of my readers who are more at ease when they can use their own discretion will now feel relieved. I share their feelings. But the free elements – fire, water and air – will not carry us unless we have first practised our steps on firm ground. We follow rules in order to make the exceptions more impressive. From the letter we distil our vision, and on turning back observe the letter with new eyes. The growing precision of our understanding should enhance, and not diminish, our sense of wonder.

(1976)

FORM AND PSYCHOLOGY IN BEETHOVEN'S
PIANO SONATAS

I should say at the outset that the remarks that follow are those of a practical musician, and they apply first and foremost to practical performance. Further, although I find it necessary and refreshing to *think* about music, I am always conscious of the fact that *feeling* must remain the Alpha and Omega of a musician; therefore my remarks proceed from feeling and return to it.

I

Beethoven's piano sonatas are unique in three respects. First, they represent the whole development of a genius, from his beginnings to the threshold of the late quartets. There the Diabelli Variations and the last set of Bagatelles round out the picture. Secondly, there is not an inferior work among them – in contrast to many of the sets of variations, for example, which tend to be uneven. I find it impossible to share Busoni's low opinion of Beethoven's early works. If we must divide Beethoven's works into three periods in line with Liszt's pronouncement 'l'adolescent, l'homme, le dieu', then the young Beethoven already stands there as a great composer. We must not take the term 'adolescent' too literally, however: after all, Beethoven was twenty-four when his Opus 1 was published. Thirdly, Beethoven does not repeat himself in his sonatas; each work, each movement is a new organism.

I like to think of every masterpiece as a phenomenon in its own right. In doing so, the usual way of looking for relationships and analogies within a certain style is of no great use to me. There are people who want to put everything into pigeon-holes: Beethoven is allowed to be fierce and heroic, but not graceful; Mozart is allowed to be graceful and crisp, but not melancholy; Bach has to be majestic; the late eighteenth century is neatly divorced from the early nineteenth, and so on. As an interpreter – that is, in my threefold function of curator, executor and obstetrician – I am not interested in clichés, but in what is special and unique.

I should like to illustrate my standpoint with two quotations. The first is from an essay by Werner Schmalenbach, the curator of one of West Germany's larger art collections. He says: 'It is not the duty of an art museum to give a documentation of art history, nor is it its duty to teach the history of art. History and style can be taught from reproductions; masterpieces have something quite different to say . . . . In a museum only artistic incomparability counts; this has nothing to do with artistic style, for works of art are thoroughly comparable in style, independent of their quality.'

Next I should like to quote Tovey, who wrote, in connection with Beethoven's Sonata Op. 54: 'It resembles all Beethoven's other works, great and small, late, middle and early, in this – that it can be properly understood only on its own terms. If Beethoven uses an old convention, we must find out how it fits the use he makes of it, instead of imagining that its origin elsewhere explains its presence here. If Beethoven writes in a form and style which cannot be found elsewhere, we must, as Hans Sachs says, find its own rules without worrying because it does not fit ours.'

Having spoken of the variety in Beethoven's sonatas, we really ought to ask ourselves what the word 'sonata' means and what interpretations the term allows. We can distinguish between three meanings: the first and oldest stands for an 'instrumental piece' as opposed to the vocal 'cantata'; the second means a cyclic work that has two or more movements without being a suite; and the third refers to the so-called 'sonata form' which was defined not earlier than 1827 by Heinrich Birnbach and later, in 1838, by Adolph Bernhard Marx. We are all familiar with the usual description of sonata form today: exposition (principal theme followed by one or more subsidiary themes in the dominant or mediant), development, recapitulation (in which the subsidiary theme returns in the tonic) and coda. This description is an over-simplification: there are plenty of sonata forms it does not measure up to, for one reason or another. For example, we find sonata forms that make do with a single theme, among them two by Beethoven: the third movement of Op. 10, No. 2 and the second movement of Op. 54. Two others of his sonatas are without sonata form entirely, namely Op. 26 and Op. 27, No. 1. On the other hand, there are two sonatas with no fewer than three sonata forms: Op. 10, No. 1[1] and Op. 31, No. 3; and a whole list of sonatas with two.

Again I should like to quote Tovey, as he draws attention to two interesting characteristics of the sonata: 'The sonata is an essentially dramatic art form, combining the emotional range and vivid presentation of a full-sized stage drama with the terseness of a short story;' and 'As the sonata forms accomplish their designs more quickly than they can satisfy their emotional issues, they retain the division into separate pieces inherited from the earlier suite forms, which are their decorative prototype.'

I quite agree with Tovey's bringing out the sonata's dramatic nature and emotional engagement as emphatically as he does. The sonata frees itself from the ceremonial attitude of the suite. It is, for fanciers of the eighteenth century, startlingly 'private'. 'Sonatas are like studies of the several mental attitudes and passions of Man,' said a certain Abbé Pluche in 1732. If we attempt to define the drama of Beethoven's sonata form more precisely, we are bound to notice that it is a drama in which the character of the principal theme predominates. Beethoven himself did speak about the 'battle between the two principles', but his remarks are rather vague, or else Schindler did not understand him quite correctly. However great the difference between the themes, however violently they may clash in the development, the character of the principal theme dominates. The principal theme reigns like a king surrounded by his court. Not until Schubert's sonatas is this maxim called into question, and the terms 'principal theme' and 'subsidiary theme' lose their meaning at times; then the themes face each other like distant planets. This enlarged field of tension was expanded still further by Liszt in his Sonata in B minor, the most powerful post-Schubert sonata structure. Here the defiance of the principal theme does not have the last word; the tranquillity of the fifth and last theme ends the piece.

[1]The second movement of Op. 10, No. 1 is a sonata form without a development section, unless one accepts the broken chord in bar 45 as the shortest development section ever written!

However, the sonata (or quartet, or symphony) did make one concession to the ceremonial at first: it took into its cycle of movements the minuet, one of the most formal of all suite movements. But here, too, the form began to evolve in a more spontaneous direction. The result was the scherzo.

Czerny is mistaken in assuming that Beethoven invented the scherzo. That honour apparently goes to Haydn, who used two kinds of scherzo or scherzando, both jocose and brisk, but different as to form and rhythm. One is in 3/4, one beat to a bar, and related to the minuet, with a contrasting trio before the literal repeat; the other is in 2/4, usually appearing as a finale, with no firm bonds to a definite form. In Beethoven's sonatas we have a 2/4 scherzo in sonata form as the second movement of the Sonata Op. 31, No. 3, but also a 3/4 scherzo in rondo form as the finale of Op. 14, No. 2. The connecting link between all the divergent forms is, as I have said, the scherzando character.

Something similar happens with the minuet. We distinguish between the actual minuet in strict minuet form, and the *tempo di minuetto,* a movement tied to no particular form, whose principal theme has minuet character. Beethoven generally underlined the formality of his minuets, and the dramatic quality of his scherzos. The minuet character in his piano works can be described in two words: *dolce* and *grazioso.* In this respect he was much more orthodox than Haydn and Mozart, whose minuets are open to practically any emotion compatible with three strict crotchet beats. We can call to mind majestic, energetic, passionate, even wild minuets (think of Mozart's Symphony in G minor); in such instances nothing more than the formal shell of the ceremonial remains. Today we unfortunately hear most minuets trip or strut along in uniform gravity.

II

Let me approach the subject of form and psychology from another angle. What do we do when we want to perceive the particular attributes of a personality as clearly as possible? We compare it to a personality of a different nature. Thus we may compare the sonata composer Beethoven with the sonata composer Schubert. In Beethoven's music we never lose our bearings, we always know where we are; Schubert, on the other hand, puts us into a dream. Beethoven composes like an architect, Schubert like a sleepwalker. This is not to say, of course, that Schubert's craftsmanship is shoddy, or that Beethoven's music remains prosaic: I mean that the attitudes of the two masters to the problems of composition were different by nature.

Before I present technical proof to support my analogies of architect and sleepwalker, I should like to talk about the difference between Classical and Romantic form, as seen by a performer. When a Classical or 'Classicistic' piece is played without any great emotional involvement but with a certain solid craftsmanship, the form of the piece can nevertheless prove to be a firm framework that will in many instances carry the performance. (There are, in fact, experts who seem to hold the view that the less the emotional involvement, the better the performance.)

Now Romantic music, performed in this way, would give a completely different result, as a rule. Only insight into the psychology of the piece can bring about the vision of form – form is disclosed by emotion.

In other words, if I compare Classical form to a drawing, anyone can see the lines and outlines of the drawing, even if he is unable to perceive what the drawing is all about. Romantic form, on the other hand, could be compared to a drawing that is invisible except to the understanding eye.

Now I should like to offer the proofs I promised. Looking at the first movements of Beethoven's sonatas (which are usually in sonata form), we notice that Beethoven generally constructs his principal themes by a technique I should like to call, for want of a better name, the technique of foreshortening. The principal theme of Op. 2, No. 1 is a simple example.

The succession of harmonies up to the fermata is foreshortened according to the following scheme: two two-bar units, two one-bar units, three half-bar units. Motivic and rhythmic foreshortenings add to the process. This technique dominates not only the thematic construction but, in a much more complex way, the organization of the whole movement.

The technique of foreshortening, or at least the rudiments of it, can be traced back via Mozart and Haydn to Bach and the Baroque chaconne. So far as I know, it is not mentioned in contemporary text-books on composition, but it must have been well known. Even the waltz theme by Diabelli that Beethoven used for his set of Variations is constructed in that technique.[1] But no one used foreshortening so consistently and with such a degree of complexity as Beethoven. I would venture to say that this is *the* driving force of his sonata forms and a basic principle of his musical thought. Later I shall say a few words about how this technique works. It gives Beethoven's music its inexorable forward drive, while Schubert's music at times almost conveys the impression of a passive state, a series of episodes communicating mysteriously with one another. Accordingly, it is not unusual for Schubert to invent his themes as a period or *Lied*.

We learn more about the architect and the sleepwalker from their treatment of harmony. Schubert was fond of daring tensions between distant keys; his predilection for chromatic neighbouring keys is notorious. The polarity of C major and C sharp minor dominates the *Wanderer* Fantasy, for example; the polarity of F minor and F sharp minor dominates the F minor Fantasy for four hands. The macabre finale of the Sonata in C minor has subsidiary sections in D flat and C sharp minor on one side, and in B major on the other. And the first movement of the unfinished Sonata in C major takes a risk that puts them all in the shade, namely a subsidiary theme starting in B minor. It often happens that chromatic neighbours appear next to one another abruptly and glaringly. Schubert strides across harmonic abysses as though by compulsion, and we cannot help remembering that sleepwalkers never lose their step.

In Beethoven a new movement or theme in a chromatic neighbouring key is unthinkable. (Before him, however, that tireless

---

[1] Instead of relying on the harmonic or melodic organization of Diabelli's waltz, Beethoven chose its foreshortened structure as the common denominator for his Thirty-three Variations, and without it would hardly have been compelled to write them at all.

adventurer Haydn had in his great Sonata in E flat major a slow movement in E major; and there is an earlier example in C.P.E. Bach.) When Beethoven does make his way to a distant key – which happens only rarely, and then with logical preparation – there are far-reaching consequences for the whole work. Recall the first movement of the *Hammerklavier* Sonata in B flat major, Op. 106: the appearance of B major in the development, and even more so the modulation to B minor in the recapitulation, give rise, as Ratz has shown, to formal and psychological problems that it takes all of the remaining movements to solve. One is tempted to say that the harmonic problems of the first movement constitute the rest of the movements and make them necessary. Incidentally, Beethoven follows a definite key symbolism in the *Hammerklavier* Sonata. An entry in one of his sketchbooks reads 'B minor, black key'. Set against it, the tonic B flat major is perceived as the key of luminous energy. Accordingly, the fugue subject is in the positive B flat major, but its retrograde form is in the negative B minor. Now, the scales of B flat major and B minor have two notes in common, G and D. The mediant keys of G major and D major negotiate between the two poles; they move in a sphere of lyrical deliverance and consolation, a sphere that becomes out-and-out religious in the second fugue subject.

III

As I said earlier, Classical form can be compared to a drawing whose lines are visible to everyone, even to those who cannot recognize what exactly the lines depict. But what do they actually depict? Anyone, presumably even someone with no musical gifts whatever, can analyse musical form with some success, provided he is taught how to follow certain intellectual mechanisms. Tracking down the character, the psychological processes of the music, however, demands talent. Beethoven's pupil Ries reports as follows about the master's piano instruction: 'If I missed something in a passage, or played wrongly the notes and leaps he often wanted me to bring out strongly, he rarely said anything; but when I fell short as regards expression, crescendos, etc., or the character of the piece, he got exasperated because, as he said, the first was an accident, but the other was a lack of judgement, feeling or attentiveness. The former happened to him quite often too, even when he played in public.' It is indicative that composers of the past were much more inclined to talk about 'expression and gusto' (Mozart), about character, atmosphere, the poetic idea and similar matters, than about the formal aspects of musical craftsmanship.

Let us look at the start of the last movement of Op. 10, No. 3. There are themes in which a lot, if not everything, depends on what the performance brings to light beneath the surface of conventional performing habits. One can play the rondo theme of Op. 10, No. 3 with academic strictness or in the spirit of an apparently improvised game of musical hide-and-seek that determines, with two important exceptions, the further sprightly progress of the piece. The first of these exceptions is the false recapitulation beginning at bar 46, which leads us to a question ('Is all this really just a joke?')

followed by a big six-bar question mark

that is resolved in the true recapitulation.

We heave a sigh of relief: it was a joke after all. But after the second energetic outburst of the movement, which seemed like an ultimate triumph of joy, serious doubts begin to crop up again fourteen bars before the end.

Then the last eight bars unite the opposing sentiments in a wonderful way: we feel happily freed from a burden, yet we sense that our doubts were not unjustified. These two episodes give the movement a poetical background that makes the torment of the slow movement legitimate in retrospect; we are assured that the torment was not suffered in vain.

As a second example, let us take the Minuet of the same sonata. We shall consider it separately at first and disregard its context within the work. We have before us a little piece in which graceful freshness alternates with sections of rustic vigour. Now let us put the four movements of the sonata together again, experiencing the bright-as-day energy of the first movement followed by the Adagio's melancholy night, which ends when the great elegy slowly dies away, and then attempt, not mechanically but with emotional involvement, to hear the Minuet grow out of it.

Is this still the healthy, unconstrained piece we said it was just a moment ago? What sensitive performer will expose us immediately to the full light of day? Will he not rather evolve the beginning of the Minuet with circumspect gentleness from the darkness of the general pause between the movements? What is the function of that general pause, anyway? Does it break the continuity between the two movements? Can the audience be permitted to move around in its seats, to relax and cough before the Minuet begins, as though nothing had happened? Anyone who believes this is impervious to the psychological side of music. The purpose of the general pause is to create a moment of motionless silence, after which the Minuet drops like balm on the wounds.

An example of a similar kind is the last movement of the Sonata Op. 26. Taken purely on its own terms, the piece reminds us of the 'Clementi-Cramer passage style', to which an unproblematic performance with emphasis on technical elegance would do justice. Within the 'psychological composition', to use the phrase Edwin Fischer applied to this sonata, the finale takes on a completely altered meaning. We would brand Beethoven a bungler or a cynic if we were to launch a brilliant *étude* after the moving coda of the familiar funeral march.

As we know, Beethoven toyed with the idea of publishing a complete edition of his works with poetic titles. It is hardly surprising that he did not do it after all. I recall a statement from an English newspaper, the *Daily Mail:* 'When I glimpse the backs of women's knees, I seem to hear the first movement of Beethoven's *Pastoral* Symphony.' I am afraid that many comments on musical character are not much more illuminating, and are less amusing. But there was probably another reason that caused Beethoven to drop the plan. The later his style, the more he tries to prevent psychological misunderstandings, the more he confirms the psychological process by procedures of form and texture up to the point where they disclose each other mutually.

A particularly good example of this is the first movement of the Sonata Op. 54. There is no conventional form to lull us. The movement begins like a minuet, with a *dolce-grazioso* theme that is emphatically feminine in nature.

The sharply contrasted second theme, with its masculine stamping octave triplets, coincides with the beginning of the trio.

In its rage it gets out of all control, winds up in A flat major to its amazement, makes a rather subdued modulation to F major and a transition to the gracefulness of the beginning. Beauty, however – I am referring to Richard Rosenberg's christening of the movement 'La Belle et la Bête' – Beauty has not remained completely unaffected by the Beast's wild behaviour: the recapitulation of the minuet has lost a bit of its naïveté; the lady puts on airs and figurations.

The trio, that is to say the triplets, appears a second time; now it is shorter and does not leave the tonic, something the Beast finds noticeably difficult – but then he must also pay his tribute to Beauty. His truculent rattling on the dominant leads straight away to the second recapitulation of the minuet.

The minuet has further gained in experience, and not only as regards figuration, for the bass progression has also changed since the beginning. Now the minuet does not begin from the repose of the tonic, but from the third – the theme, so to speak, has been shaken to its foundations.

has become

Passing minor harmonies cast little sad shadows on the comedy. Beginning at bar 128, the recapitulation expands into a foreshortening that faintly reminds us of the trio's stamping sequences, without, however, taking on the rhythm of the quaver triplets.

The sequences resolve into a chain of trills that runs out in an improvisatory passage. The lovely coda unites the feminine and masculine elements. Beauty's face appears transformed: from a motive of the minuet a new lyrical idea emerges.

Of the Beast, however, nothing more than the triplet rhythm remains, and we hear it rumbling quietly in the bass. Not only has the Beast been tamed, but he has become part of Beauty. There is, however, one last outburst of beastliness, as a result of which the Beast finally loses his identity. Triplets are resolved into duplets. The movement's end is feminine.

What has happened in this strange piece of music? The two principles that would have nothing to do with each other at the beginning
have become inseparable at the end. As we see, the psychological
process establishes the form of the movement, but the form itself is
also cast in such a way that one can deduce from it the psychological
process. Again we detect an antagonism between Beethoven and
Schubert. Schubert trusts the directness of his emotions so much that
he makes the weight of his formal organization as light as possible. In
contrast, Beethoven creates the firmest intellectual basis imaginable,
so that the emotions can emerge from it more clearly, distinctly and
unequivocally.

IV

This intellectual basis would be unthinkable without the technique of
foreshortening. I should like to draw attention to precisely this
aspect of Beethoven's form, and for two reasons: first, so far as I
know, it has been noticed only in a rudimentary way, and with no
general application; second, it can be of great practical value to the
performer.

The principle of foreshortening progressively tightens the musical
texture. It can achieve this in several different ways and combina-
tions of ways. Whole sections can be foreshortened; there are
foreshortened phrases or parts of phrases, foreshortened successions
of rhythmic values or rhythmic sections, foreshortened harmonic
progressions (often combined with rhythmic foreshortening), tightened melodic structure and tempo, tightened accents and dynamic
progressions. It usually happens that several foreshortening processes are superimposed, that they interlock or overlap. The continuity of the total process is determined by the combination and
symbiosis of various foreshortenings, so that in the course of a whole
movement, except for a few significant cæsuras, one or another of the
foreshortening elements is constantly intensified. As a rule, subsidiary themes are more foreshortened than principal themes; the
rhythmic subdivisions are often denser, the motivic components
briefer, or the harmonic progression is closer. This does not mean,
however (as I have already shown), that the character of the subsidiary theme is necessarily more agitated than that of the principal
theme. The reverse can as easily be the case. When I talk about con-

tinuous foreshortening, tightening or intensification, I do not mean
to suggest a crescendo of any kind (although such foreshortening
may occur too, for example in the inversion of the Fugue in Op. 110).
The variety of the elements that make up the foreshortening process
means that there is room for every change of mood, every contrast,
every conceivable emotion.

I should like to explain the mechanism of two foreshortening fac-
tors in more detail. The rhythmic organization gets tighter when
notes on strong beats are followed by syncopations (or vice versa),
when duplets are followed by triplets, minims by crotchets, quavers
by semiquavers, and so on; the last step in rhythmic foreshortening is
the trill. The melodic organization gets tighter in roughly the following order, assuming that the rhythmic values remain constant:
1) broken chords; 2) diatonic neighbouring notes; 3) chromatic
figuration; 4) repeated notes. Repeated notes, however, lead a kind
of Jekyll and Hyde double life. If we listen to the energy of each
separate note, there is a high degree of tension; if we hear the repetition as one sustained note, there is minimum tension. In that case one
could place repeated notes at the head of the list. The function of
repeated notes, then, can be given a new interpretation: it can be the
end of an evolution and the beginning of a new one at the same time.
(Reinterpretations play an important part in the foreshortening process altogether.) We can study rhythmic and melodic aspects of
foreshortening quite clearly in the last movement of the Sonata Op.
109. The first half of variation 6 is filled with rhythmic foreshortenings; the last half is devoted principally to melodic tightening in constant demisemiquaver motion. As an introduction to the general
foreshortening process I shall give a brief analysis of the first movement of Op. 2, No. 1.[1]

The application of the foreshortening technique is not limited to
sonata forms. I should like to end with two examples, one from a
fugue, the other from a set of variations, thus showing how Beethoven bent this technique also to his psychological purposes.

Let us look first at the Sonata Op. 110. Here the Arioso dolente
and the Fugue form a unit which finds its analogy on another level, a
half-step lower, in the *Ermattete Klage* ('Exhausted Lament') and the
inversion of the Fugue. The Arioso's falling from A flat to G is as

[1]See 'The Process of Foreshortening in the First Movement of Beethoven's Sonata Op. 2, No.
1', p. 154.

expressive of exhaustion as is the lamenter's short, fitful breathing; he can no longer summon the strength to span an extensive melodic phrase. We are led to the brink of death and then witness 'the gradual resurgence of the heartbeat' (Edwin Fischer) in the crescendo on the repeated G major chords. *L'istesso tempo della Fuga poi a poi di nuovo vivente* is written over the inversion of the Fugue. Editors of the sonata have interpreted this in several ways. Some apply it to the tempo of the Fugue, others to the dynamics. For me, however, these words draw attention to the compositional process; from here to the end of the work, as it happens, the Fugue is constructed as one continuous foreshortening. And something else happens too: as the foreshortening progresses, the fugal bonds are gradually shaken off; polyphony is transformed into homophony. Vincent d'Indy called the Fugue of Op.110 an 'exertion of will to banish suffering'.

Now let us turn to the conclusion of the Sonata Op. 111. Its two movements are thesis and antithesis. Whether one speaks in terms of the real and the mystical world, of Sansara and Nirvana (Bülow), of resistance and submission (Lenz), or of the masculine and feminine principle – in any event we have the impression of a final statement.

The polarity of motion and repose is reflected in the choice of forms. The forms with the greatest tension and activity are sonata and fugue; the first movement of Op. 111 is a sonata form interlaced with fugal elements. The form of repose and steadfastness amid change is the variation form – or at least it was until Beethoven developed a new concept of variation form in his Diabelli Variations. The Adagio of Op. 111 is a set of variations in progressive rhythmic foreshortening – that is, each variation is rhythmically more tightly organized than its predecessor. (Variation movements of this kind have been known since the Baroque chaconne. I would just mention two of Mozart's finales, namely those of the Piano Concertos in G major, K 453, and in C minor, K 491.)

Only once does the Adagio of Op. 111 move away from the tonic C major. This occurrence coincides with the inner climax of the movement. At the same time, the foreshortening process is suspended and then begun again. I am talking about the cadenza-like passage that grows out of the fourth variation, after the material of this variation has been so foreshortened that it has had to resolve into a trill (bar 106). With the modulation to the dominant of E flat major we reach the focus of mystical experience. The *sf* entrance of the B flat in the bass (bar 116) starts a new foreshortening process which leads into variation 5 as though into a recapitulation, and lasts until the end. The fifth and sixth returns of the theme make possible further foreshortenings in comparison to the fourth. Schenker's sketch of the rhythmic intensification of the variations demonstrates this:

Var. 1:	3 times each	♪. = ♫♩	i.e. 3 × 3 = 9 notes
Var. 2:	3 times each	♫ = ♫♩	i.e. 3 × 4 = 12 notes
Var. 3:	3 times each	♫ = ♬♬	i.e. 3 × 8 = 24 notes
Var. 4:	3 times each	♬ = ♬♬♬	i.e. 3 × 9 = 27 notes

Variation 5 keeps up the motion of 27 notes to a bar, but the demi-semiquavers are now moving the bass line and bringing about closer changes of harmony. The last, transfigured vision of the theme is accompanied by a trill. An epilogue of six bars leads to the closing chord; its entrance on a weak beat, and the foreshortenings that led all the way to it, hardly permit an idea of finality. This chord does not close something off; rather it opens up the silence that follows, a silence we now perceive to be more important than the sound that preceded it.

(1970)

SCHUBERT

SCHUBERT'S PIANO SONATAS, 1822-1828

It is only recently that Schubert has been recognized as one of the great piano composers and one of the supreme masters of the sonata. We are indebted for this to Artur Schnabel and, in Germany, to Eduard Erdmann, who, as performers and influential teachers, opened the road to future generations. But they were isolated cases within their time. In 1928, the year of the centenary of Schubert's death, Rachmaninov, the celebrated pianist, admitted to César Saerchinger that he had not realized sonatas by Schubert existed. Even today, some older musicians continue to show a surprising amount of ignorance, doubt and contempt where Schubert's sonatas are concerned. Thus, it seems fitting to examine certain of the prejudices that still prevail against these works, in the hope of providing clues as to their neglect.

Prejudice 1: 'Schubert's style did not develop'

The reason for this belief can be found in the fact that, in spite of O. E. Deutsch's catalogue, many people have still not discovered the chronology of Schubert's output. The order in which Schubert's works were published and provided with opus numbers has little or nothing to do with the order of their composition. With the exception of his four-hand music, for which the contemporary demand must have been astounding, only a few of Schubert's major instrumental works were published during his lifetime: not more than three of the sonatas (Op. 42, 53 and 78), along with the C major Fantasy, the Moments Musicaux, and the first two of the Impromptus. The rest of the Impromptus were not published until ten years after Schubert's death, when the publisher changed the key and time signature of No. 3, transposing it from G flat to G, and omitted a couple of repeats in the opening Impromptu of the second set, Op. 142.

One can distinguish roughly two main periods in Schubert's instrumental music. The first ends in 1819 and contains the first six symphonies and fifteen piano sonatas, eleven of which remained fragments. There follows a three-year gap in Schubert's instrumental production, during which time he concentrated mainly (and unsuccessfully) on composing *Singspiele,* a kind of German opera, while, of course, the flow of Lieder never stopped. Apart from sketches for an E minor symphony, the only instrumental work composed during this time was the movement for string quartet in C minor of 1820, which already foreshadows his later, 'mature' style – that of the period starting in the autumn of 1822 and terminated by his death. The masterpieces of this period are the last eight sonatas, the last three string quartets, both piano trios, the Octet, the String Quintet, and the Unfinished and Great C major symphonies, as well as all the important four-hand works.

With the exception of a few pieces written for virtuoso display in the concert hall, such as some of the violin music and the Variations on 'Trockene Blumen' for flute and piano, nearly all of these compositions are on the same high level of accomplishment. By comparison, the compositions of the earlier period are of lesser importance, although they include such delightful works as the earlier symphonies, the *Trout* Quintet, and the smaller of the A major sonatas, which in many editions is mistaken for a later work of 1825. In these works, Schubert can be seen as a young composer gradually and playfully exploring large forms. He has not yet come to terms with Beethoven and he sees no necessity to rush his fences. When one looks at the Unfinished Symphony and the *Wanderer* Fantasy, which he composed in the autumn of 1822, the impression is strikingly different. That his venereal disease supposedly started at the same time may well be a coincidence, and I do not wish to add new myth to old prejudice; but it is not too difficult to imagine that the shock of this illness made Schubert gather his forces with almost desperate intensity, faced as he was with the possibility that the span of his life might be limited.

The later sonatas start with the rigidly concentrated A minor, Op. 143, in three movements, which closely follows the *Wanderer* Fan-

tasy. Then we have a middle group of four sonatas, composed between 1824 and 1826, comprising the C major Sonata (the last two
movements of which were thankfully left unfinished), the great four-
movement A minor, Op. 42, the D major, Op. 53 (with the strange,
not completely convincing innocence of its finale), and the dreamy G
major, Op. 78. Finally, the three sonatas of 1828, in C minor, A, and
B flat.

Let me give a few general characteristics of Schubert's later
sonatas.

The first movement is always composed in sonata form and covers
a wide emotional range. The tempo is more often moderate than fast.
In the works of 1824 and 1825 the subsidiary theme is conceived as a
variant of the principal theme.

Sonata in C major (D 840), first movement

Sonata in A minor, Op. 42 (D 845), first movement

Grand Duo in C major (D 812), first movement

The idea of monothematic composition, more fully realized in the *Wanderer* Fantasy, influenced Liszt and found its consequence in the dodecaphonic technique.

Expositions and recapitulations are nearly identical. To observe the repeat of the exposition is therefore in some cases not only superfluous, but positively damaging. There is only one sonata, the D major, where the repeat is indispensable; in three others it is optional, because the presentation of the material is more terse (A minor, Op. 143, A minor, Op. 42, and C minor).

The arbitrariness of some classical repeats will already be familiar to those who are acquainted with Haydn's sonatas. Beethoven, in some of his Diabelli Variations, leaves the most obvious considerations of proportion aside and omits repeats where the music is based on uniform patterns of rhythm sustained throughout the whole variation. I wonder how the experienced master felt about his much earlier work, the Sonata Op. 10, No. 2: he must have found the opening movement's second repeat unnecessary on account of the extreme simplicity of the material in the development.

The player at home may happily indulge in repeating the exposition of a Schubert sonata a dozen times for his private pleasure. In the concert hall he will be wise to consider that the perception of the audience, as well as his own concentration, should not be overtaxed.

That repeats are inevitably a matter of proportion is nothing more than a fashionable belief. Nor does it always follow from the inclusion of new material in those bars which especially lead back to the beginning that the composer counted on the execution of the repeat. In the case of the B flat Sonata, which is the most frequently lamented example, I am particularly happy to miss those transitional bars, so utterly unconnected is their jerky outburst to the entire movement's logic and atmosphere.

Recapitulations are followed by important codas which sum up the essence of the piece.

The title page of Czerny's piano duet arrangement of Beethoven's *Kreutzer* Sonata (see p. 23).

The opening bars of 'Wasserfluth' from *Die Winterreise*.
Above: Schubert's manuscript; below: the first print (see p. 70).

The second movement is most often an andante. It moves forward with the step and spirit of an idealized dance. This dance-like character is missing in the adagios of the *Wanderer* Fantasy (brooding) and the C minor Sonata (quiet, hymn-like), and in the Con moto of the D major Sonata, which is so often played at a funeral pace. If not in variation form, the second movement invariably follows the same scheme: it has three or five sections (ABA, ABABA); the contrasting section is always more agitated – in the late works sometimes as if shaken by fever. The motion of section B is usually continued in the reprise of A. Towards the end of the movement at least part of the opening theme may be stated in its initial simplicity.

The third movement is a scherzo or fluent minuet, the trio being a *Ländler.* Only the last two sonatas abandon the Viennese character of the trio. The Sonata Op. 143 makes do without such a movement.

The motion of the finale may be graceful, sprightly, or frighteningly macabre. This last type is a Schubert speciality; we find these dances of death in the D minor and G major string quartets and in the A minor, Op. 143, and C minor sonatas. The rhythm of many of Schubert's finales shows Spanish or Hungarian influence. The final movements of the last three sonatas are more expansive and contain literal recapitulations, while the idiom of their slow movements has ceased to be 'alpine'. There are, in fact, only two instances in these works where the local colour is identifiably Viennese: the trios of the minuets of the C minor and A major sonatas.

Prejudice 2: 'Schubert modelled his sonatas on Beethoven's and failed'

Schubert worshipped Beethoven. On his deathbed, he asked his friends not only for more of Fenimore Cooper's books, but also for a performance of Beethoven's Quartet in C sharp minor, Op. 131, which had been published the previous year, but had not yet been performed. To hear this work must have been Schubert's last deep joy. And later, in his delirium, he was reported to have said, 'Take me away from here, from under the earth. Beethoven does not lie here.' But though he venerated Beethoven, Schubert was not overwhelmed by Beethoven's greatness. He admired the master far too much to challenge him on his own terms. And he must have been keenly aware of the basic differences in their temperaments, minds, and backgrounds. As I have written elsewhere, compared to Beethoven the architect, Schubert composed like a sleepwalker. In Beethoven's sonatas we never lose our bearings; they justify themselves at all times. Schubert's sonatas happen. There is something disarmingly naïve in the way they happen.

Yet I do not want to imply that Schubert's music is primitive, let alone amateurish. Schubert's naïveté leaves room for a good deal of sophistication, as did Haydn's, and for a marvellous variety of mood, colour and texture. Therefore, to accept all-out simplicity as a cardinal virtue of the Schubert player is to accept an over-simplification; it would turn the music of a great composer into minor music. Just in case a warning is needed, let me quote Tovey: 'Nothing is more false than the doctrine that great music cannot be ruined in performance.' This prejudice belongs to the family of popular statements like 'There are no bad pianos, only bad pianists' or 'There are no bad orchestras, only bad conductors.'

It may well be that this 'accidental' quality in Schubert's sonatas is one of the main reasons why they are so dearly loved by present-day musicians and have been so much more readily accepted by the public within the last decades, along with Mahler's symphonies. The music of these two composers does not set self-sufficient order against chaos. Events do not unfold with graceful or grim logic; they could have taken another turn at many points. We feel not masters but victims of the situation. This reflects for many of us the experience of living in a world in which the exponential growth of problems seems to defy all conceivable solutions. Mahler, by the way, is known to have played Schubert's D major Sonata for his friends in Leipzig in 1887. The second idea in the last movement, bars 30-32, strikes us as typically 'Mahlerian'.

If we look in Schubert's sonatas for Beethoven's virtues, we shall find them full of flaws; they will seem formless, too long, too lyrical, and harmonically overspiced. We should, instead, concentrate on the basic differences of their styles.

In my essay 'Form and Psychology in Beethoven's Piano Sonatas' I have already examined some evidence of Beethoven's logical energy as compared to Schubert's more random and episodic writing. As I showed there, Beethoven's music is dominated by the technique of foreshortening, the propelling dynamism of which organizes not only thematic details, but entire movements. He seems determined to create the firmest intellectual basis in order to make all matters of emotional character as unmistakable as possible. Schubert puts more trust in the directness of his emotions. He seems almost afraid of too much intellectual weight and rigour. Economy to him is hardly a matter of prime importance. And over all its prodigious emotional range, his music remains mysteriously episodic.

The resemblance of the beginning of Schubert's C minor Sonata to Beethoven's theme for his C minor Variations has often been quoted as proof of Beethoven's influence on Schubert. Yet it seems to me that the similarities of these two openings are less revealing than their differences.

Beethoven: Variations in C minor (1806)

Sonata in C minor (D 958), first movement

In Beethoven's theme the opening bars give rise to expectations which, by the use of foreshortening, the concluding bars precisely fulfil. Schubert disappoints our structural expectations as early as bar 6. From here to bar 12 the music tries, but does not manage, to leave the ground. Schubert's bass is tied to the basic C until the transition which precedes the subsidiary theme in E flat starts to move away from reality to illusion. If Schubert has set out to create foreshortening in Beethoven's manner, he has failed. The question is, however, whether the foreshortening was meant to succeed, or whether its failure gives us a psychological clue. If we look at the course of events in this movement, we find that the initial feeling of despair is maintained. The structure of the theme justifies itself in retrospect. It gives the impression less of majestic grandeur than of panic. The leading character in this tragedy is being chased and cornered, and looks in vain for a way of escape.

Whenever Beethoven attempted to convey a similar atmosphere of panic – we might think of his *Sonate Pathétique* – he would, at the same time, offer consolation by adhering to his structural logic. Even in his most chaotic moments Beethoven chose (or could not help) to represent order, whereas the music Schubert composed in the middle section of the Andante of the great A major Sonata comes amazingly close to being chaos itself.

The same A major Sonata's last movement is strikingly related to the Rondo of Beethoven's Op. 31, No. 1. As both Charles Rosen and Edward T. Cone have observed, Schubert made very accurate use not only of Beethoven's general formal design, but also of many individual details of construction. Yet the result does not easily give its secret away. Schubert has significantly changed the proportion of sections, and his finale is distinctly different in atmosphere and a great deal wider in its emotional range.

In 1828 Schubert must have felt secure enough to learn from Beethoven without losing his identity. Any listener to Schubert's Rondo who did not know Beethoven's would by no means be reminded of Beethoven's style; he would probably consider it a particularly pure example of Schubert's instrumental lyricism. The listener to Beethoven's Rondo, on the other hand, unfamiliar with Schubert's, and unaware of the chronology, might find this movement more 'Schubertian' than anything this composer wrote, with the possible exception of the Rondo from the Sonata Op. 90. As it happens, this is the only other of Beethoven's pieces whose layout

Schubert seems to have deliberately used as a model; his A major Rondo for piano duet, also of 1828, follows its formal pattern with similar liberties, and results.

Where Schubert modelled his music on Beethoven's, he succeeded.

Prejudice 3: 'Schubert's music is like the soft, comforting contours of the Austrian landscape'

Whoever invented this description seems to have missed the bizarre, majestic and forbidding aspects of the Austrian countryside. The image of Schubert's music as being genial, pleasing, mellow and sentimental stems from the times when his melodies were misused in operettas. Schubert could be all these, though he seems to me very rarely sentimental. But he could be so many other things besides. Like all truly great composers, he defies pigeon-holing. It was Artur Schnabel who, in an article for the *Musical Courier* in 1928, pointed out that Schubert was no mere melodist, but a composer of intensely dramatic sonatas. Schubert's range of expression was miraculously wide. His dynamic indications alone belie the mellow lyricist: not only in his piano works does he expand previous dynamic limits to *ppp* and *fff*; following the example of Weber, whose E flat Polonaise of 1808 has *fff*, also songs like *Der Doppelgänger* give evidence of Schubert's craving for the extreme, encompassing mere whisper and frenzied shriek. His emotional scope as a sonata composer leads us from the severe determination of the Sonata Op. 143 to the roaming, quasi-improvising freedom of the first two movements of the great A major, which culminate in the feverish paroxysm of the Andante's middle section, leaving conventional construction so far behind that it needed Schoenberg to surpass its degree of anarchy in the third of his Piano Pieces, Op. 11.

Prejudice 4: 'Schubert's piano works are "unpianistic" '

An accusation like this seems slightly ludicrous to me at a time when pianists have accepted *Petruschka* and the unsurpassable pianistic perversions of Brahms's Second Piano Concerto. Who, in all seriousness, would compare such challenges to the few pages of the D major,

C minor and C major sonatas, where Schubert forces onto the piano ideas which would be more comfortably executed on other instruments? Schumann, by the way, was full of praise for Schubert's sonorous piano style, which 'seems to come from the depths of the pianoforte'. However, his piano music neither idolizes the facile performer nor respects the limitations of the instrument. Schubert himself was not a very brilliant player; he does not seem to have owned a piano and would hardly have had the time to practise anyway. Nevertheless, his instinct for the possibilities of the instrument was powerful, though it was rarely used for its own sake. I recall a recital at New York's Carnegie Hall, where a piano student said to his girl friend, after a performance of the G major Sonata, 'I don't dig it. It's all music.'

Schubert's piano style is no less orchestral than it is vocal. In the *Wanderer* Fantasy, the piano is turned into an orchestra much more radically than had ever been done before; not only the individual colours of orchestral instruments are evoked, but also the full blast of the *tutti*. If you try to play the *Wanderer* Fantasy and Beethoven's Sonata Op. 106 on a piano of the 1820s, you will realize how much more Schubert's piece depended on the instruments of the future to come alive. Much the same applies to his Great C major Symphony in comparison with Beethoven's Ninth. The *Wanderer* Fantasy influenced Liszt decisively, not only in its approach toward piano sound and its demands on the stamina of the player, but also in its monothematic construction. The sonatas of 1823 to 1826 continue an orchestral style of writing which employs tremoli, fast octaves, and repetitions. The first movement of the Unfinished C major Sonata comes closest to a piano reduction of a symphonic movement; and the D major Sonata suggests to us the possibility that the Great C major Symphony in a first version may also have been composed at Gastein in 1825. The last three sonatas, on the other hand, seem more like disguised string quintets, and they were written in the year of the String Quintet, 1828, shortly before Schubert died.

We must ask ourselves whether these are works destined for another medium which found their way to the piano by mistake. We find the answer when we compare Liszt's transcription of the *Wanderer* Fantasy for piano and orchestra with a good performance of the original version: the latter is the more convincing. Schubert evokes an orchestra, a chamber music group, or a Lieder singer on the piano, but he does it in pianistic terms. The opening of the second movement of the B flat Sonata may serve as an example.

One could imagine this opening played by a string quartet with pizzicato bass notes, and indeed I have heard a pianist who tried to perform it that way. But this is a misunderstanding: the pedal has to give
the mild glow to the *pp* cantilena of the two violins (or singers), which
would otherwise sound rather pale and unsustained, while the accompanying figure adds to the *cantabile* quality and makes it dynamically
more vibrant. Even if Schubert in his manuscript had not given one of
his rare pedal indications at the beginning of the line, we would know
from the layout of the sound that the pedal has to maintain the
harmonies through each bar. There are many other instances of short
bass notes held by the pedal, as for example in this passage from the
second movement of the *Wanderer* Fantasy:

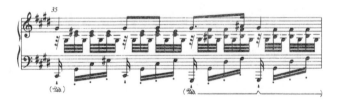

In Schubert's piano music – as also in Liszt's – Anton Rubinstein's
assertion that the pedal is the soul of the piano comes true. Without
the controlled, generous and inspired use of the pedal, Schubert's
music remains buried within the conventional self-containment of the
piano which he left behind. Unfortunately, Schubert's notation is
often misunderstood in this respect. There are two possible methods
of notation: either the composer writes down how long the note
should sound, or he indicates how long the finger should or can be
kept on the key. We could call these the musical notation and the
technical notation. The two can, but do not have to be, identical,
because the pedal can make the sound continue after the finger has
left the key. Schubert's notation is technical. The value of the notes,
as Schubert wrote them down, does not always apply to the duration
of sound as musically necessary.

As Schubert's pedal markings are a good deal sparser even than Beethoven's, it is left to the imagination of the player where the pedal has to help the notation. If I were to play, for instance, bars 33/34 from the second movement of the C major Sonata (D 840)

without the necessary pedal, it would introduce an alien character to the context – it would sound grotesque rather than grand – and it would lose its orchestral richness. Now this is a fairly clear case of sustained bass notes where the fingers could not hold the keys. The opening of the second movement of the D major Sonata is an example of where the fingers *should* not hold the keys, even though they would be available to do so.

Its staccato chords have probably to be understood plus pedal: Schubert wrote the word *legato* on top of the first bar. It may be surprising to those who are not experienced pianists to learn that it makes a difference whether we play staccato, portato, or legato within the pedal; but it does colour the sound differently and retains some of the characteristics of *secco* articulation. Generally, however, when Schubert wants detached notes tied by pedal, he puts dots *and* slurs: ⌢.

Among the innovations Schubert introduced into piano literature is the expressive use of string tremoli, as in the second movement of the *Wanderer* Fantasy

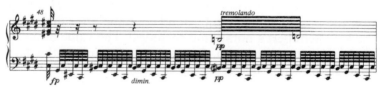

or in the first of the Posthumous Pieces. Schubert writes them down in the simplest possible manner. But his notation should not be more than a point of departure for the imagination of the player. It is essential to adapt the tremolo figures in the first movement of the Sonata Op. 143, for instance, so as to bring out their musical meaning and orchestral colour. Here, as so often, the performer should imagine himself to be a conductor rather than a pianist.

Renderings of tremolo figures that are all too literal may be the reason for the belief that tremoli are badly suited to the piano. It should be remembered that Liszt delighted in tremoli all his life, whether he used them in an orchestral manner in *Vallée d'Obermann*, as an imitation of the cimbalom in his Eleventh Hungarian Rhapsody, or as a poetic evocation of water in *Les jeux d'eau à la Villa d'Este.*

Schubert was still a young composer when he died. He was not used to hearing his instrumental works performed. To quote John Reed: 'The piano sonata had an old-fashioned air about it. Public performance of a piano sonata was a very rare event (only one of Beethoven's sonatas, it is said, was performed publicly in his lifetime), and in the domestic market the demand was all for fantasies, dances, duet pieces ("brilliant, but not too difficult") and trivial salon pieces.' Schubert's notation did not always develop the practical clarity of that of Beethoven's middle and late years. Like Mozart's, his notation is that of a *cantabile* composer, a string player, or singer. Mozart and Schubert have in common the trait that their melodic invention is often vocal. Mozart was criticized by Nägeli, one of the leading writers on music at the beginning of the nineteenth century, because his instrumental music was not, like Haydn's, purely enough instrumental; Nägeli called it too operatic. In Schubert's music we hear the Lieder singer (in the last movement of the A major Sonata, D 959), the narrator (in the opening of the A minor Sonata, Op. 42), or the rather strange combination of a narrating male choir (in the opening of the second movement of the D major Sonata).

It is not enough to imagine Schubert's melodies sung or fiddled: we have to translate their *cantabile* into pianistic terms. The main problem is the understanding of accents. *Cantabile* accents often cannot be played on the piano as positive accents, that is, as isolated louder notes. They usually have to be prepared, and lend some, or even most, of their emphasis to the upbeat; or they can be made meaningful by a change of colour (balance); or an accompaniment figure can discreetly suggest an increase in intensity within the accented note. Schubert was an accent maniac. Some of his accents are negligible: I prefer the beginning of the Great C major Symphony without obvious accents in the horn.

Some of Schubert's notation habits are surprisingly old-fashioned. His writing of appoggiaturas in his songs has fortunately been taken care of since Friedländer's edition and cannot do much more harm. But there is hardly a composer after the Baroque age whose rhythm is so frequently 'mis-spelt'. Whenever Schubert wants to use triplets in a quadruplet time scheme he writes not ♩³♪ , but ♫♪ . This rhythm, then, has often to be adjusted to its rhythmic surroundings in the Baroque manner.

'Wasserfluth'

Neither the manuscript nor the first print of the song 'Wasserfluth' from *Die Winterreise* (see plate facing p. 61) leaves the slightest doubt that the Brahmsian polyrhythm usually produced is wrong: the dotted rhythm has to be adjusted to the triplets where they occur together and, I should like to add, most probably where it stands alone as well.

From my experience of Schubert's works, and my knowledge of manuscripts and first prints, I am inclined to think that the adjustment of dotted rhythms, even in slower tempi, is the rule, and polyrhythm the exception. (If there is any evidence for soft contours in Schubert's music, here it is.) In the middle section of the slow movement of the B flat Sonata, the dotted rhythm has to go with the sextuplet.

There are, however, a fair number of exceptions and doubtful cases. One of the exceptions seems to be in the Adagio of the C minor

Sonata, where an adjustment of the demisemiquavers in bar 29 ff. would diminish the feeling of continuity established before, and weaken the sinister impact of the following octave leaps,

whereas the later episode after the first recapitulation of the opening theme (bar 62 ff.), with its continuous triplets, demands adjustment for as long as the triplets last (bar 78), again for the reason that greater continuity is thereby suggested until the accompaniment switches to demisemiquavers and gives the signal for the dotted rhythm to take over.

Schubert was not the last composer to write 'dotted triplets'. There are plenty of them in Schumann's first Novelette and particularly in Chopin's *Polonaise-Fantaisie*.

For the musician dealing with Schubert's sonatas, another practical hazard is that some of the editions are full of mistakes. The necessity of using a text which cleanly reproduces Schubert's original manuscripts, or the first prints where they are relevant, or both, cannot be stressed enough, even if this text at some points is only raw material for the performer. So far there are two relatively reliable *Urtext* editions, by Henle and Universal. Others being prepared are by Bärenreiter and Oxford University Press. The Lea pocket scores, which have the word *Urtext* on the cover, are in fact merely a reproduction of Breitkopf & Härtel's old 'Complete Edition' with its abundance of alterations and mistakes.

The problem starts with Schubert himself. If Beethoven has been called a bad proof-reader, Schubert, in the case of the first print of his *Wanderer* Fantasy and his Sonata Op. 42, appears to have been no proof-reader at all. After the rediscovery of the manuscript, at least the text of the *Wanderer* Fantasy has been restored in recent editions. The manuscript of Op. 42 unfortunately is missing: it thus remains our not too demanding task to recompose the four bars which were left out by mistake in the first variation of the second movement, as they are still missing in all modern editions. Paul Badura-Skoda was the first to comment on these bars; he has also pointed out a missing bar of rest in the finale, after bar 154, and I should like to add to the list of mistakes a wrong octave in variation 4 (bar 114) of the Andante, where the fourth octave in the left hand should read G instead of F.

In the second movement of the G major Sonata, manuscript and first edition differ in one important point: of eight turns which adorn the theme and its recapitulations in the manuscript, seven are omitted in the first print. Is it fair to blame the engraver for so many omissions? It seems much more likely that Schubert had second thoughts before the sonata went into print – it was one of the three published during his lifetime – and left out the turns where they are unnecessary. Once one becomes familiar with the unadorned version of the theme, these turns sound irritatingly conventional. Only the extensively ornamented first recapitulation asks for turns, and only here, so I believe, has the engraver omitted the first of the two (bar 82) by mistake. If I had not checked the first print, I would never have discovered the discrepancy: both modern *Urtext* editions present all the turns according to the manuscript. One edition omits any reference to the matter, while the information provided by the other is incomplete and misleading.

All printed texts of the later A major Sonata give a wrong reading of bars 7 and 8 of the Scherzo, owing to errors in Schubert's manuscript; a sketch for the movement in the Vienna Municipal Library shows the right notes.

should read

Most performances of the D major Sonata, including Schnabel's, follow the distortions of the Breitkopf & Härtel edition, with its two excess bars, one in the second and one in the fourth movement, apart from a large number of wrong notes and wrong or missing dynamic markings.

Finally, I should like to go back to my starting point and ask: Why has Schubert been neglected as an instrumental composer? Here is a short list of reasons.

1) The neglect originated in Schubert's lifetime. Schubert's personal appearance was unprepossessing and without self-confidence. There was no visible sign of the genius.

2) Schubert was neither a solo concert performer nor a teacher who would pass on a tradition of performance.

3) Apart from his four-hand music, most of his instrumental works were not published and performed until long after the composer's death. The Great C major Symphony (if we are to believe John Reed) was rehearsed in Vienna in its first version in 1826, but put aside because of its length and difficulty. In 1839 another performance was attempted, but at the first rehearsal the musicians refused to carry out the necessary number of rehearsals for the whole work. In the same year, in Mendelssohn's Leipzig performance, the work was considerably cut. The first complete performance took place in Vienna in 1850.

4) Vogl, the singer, convinced the audience of the Schubertiads of Schubert's genius as a Lieder composer. The view of Schubert as a miniaturist, and his youth, seemed to preclude the ability to master big forms. Grillparzer's text for the inscription on Schubert's tombstone can be taken as the opinion of Schubert's friends: 'Music buried here a noble property, but far more beautiful hopes.'

5) The Classicism of music lovers. Schubert's expansive, static, and often unpredictable music contradicted Beethoven's structural power, or Mendelssohn's easy clarity.

6) The Romanticism of music lovers. They mistrusted the use of apparently conventional musical forms.

7) Schubert's piano works often surpassed the possibilities of his instruments, as the Great C major Symphony surpassed the size and performing habits of contemporary orchestras. To play many lines of difficult and 'ungratifying' accompaniment in its final movement caused a wave of protest among the second violins.

8) The Vienna of the 1820s indulged in a Rossini craze and adored the easy-going. Later, in 1839, when two movements of the Great C

major Symphony were finally played, there was an aria from Donizetti's *Lucia di Lammermoor* performed in between. Of the important Schubert pioneers, only Brahms was connected with Vienna; Schumann, Mendelssohn, Liszt, George Grove – none of them was Viennese. To see four of the great composers of the nineteenth century among Schubert's most faithful admirers ought to impress those who persist in the belief that Schubert, though gifted, was not sufficiently professional. As a fitting conclusion, I should like to quote Liszt, who said of Schubert: 'Such is the spell of your emotional world that it very nearly blinds us to the greatness of your craftsmanship.' (*Fast lässest Du die Grösse Deiner Meisterschaft vergessen ob dem Zauber Deines Gemütes.*)

(1974)

LISZT

LISZT MISUNDERSTOOD

I

I know I am compromising myself by speaking up for Liszt. Audiences in Central Europe, Holland and Scandinavia tend to be irritated by the sight of Liszt's name on a concert bill. If one should happen to play a Beethoven sonata in the same programme, they are apt to shut their ears, as it were, and project onto that performance all the prejudices they have against Liszt: his alleged bombast, superficiality, cheap sentimentality, formlessness, his striving after effect for effect's sake. For, so the audience reckons, a pianist who champions Liszt cannot be taken seriously as an interpreter of the Classics. People forget that Liszt himself was the foremost Beethoven interpreter of his century. It would be more to the point if they were to adopt the opposite approach and accept as an outstanding Liszt player only a pianist who had proved his competence in the interpretation of Classical masterpieces.

So pianists tend to warn one another to avoid performances of Liszt in Amsterdam or Vienna, Munich or Stockholm. Yet in the rest of the world, east and west alike, his piano music continues to cast its spell, although even so one still finds a weakness for a certain type of virtuoso who, unmindful of Classical rules, seems to be at his best whenever – to put it bluntly – the greatest possible number of notes has to be crowded into the shortest possible space of time. Composers as dissimilar as Liszt and Rachmaninov are sometimes mentioned in the same breath, as if genius and the art of elevated conversation were only one step apart. When the difference between a great man and a *grand seigneur* is so lightly ignored, one must regard any enthusiasm for Liszt with caution.

II

Liszt's musical idiom has been claimed as part of their own by the Hungarians, Germans and French. His love of French poetry and culture – at one time personified, rather imperfectly, by Marie d'Agoult – is as familiar to us as that passion for the Romantic vision of Hungary which addressed his senses chiefly through its gipsy music. Though it would be an exaggeration to say that the Hungarian Rhapsodies occupy as central a place within his *œuvre* as do the Mazurkas and Polonaises in Chopin's life work, the role played by the gipsy scale in Liszt's compositions from the Weimar period onwards should not be underrated. The musical language of both Berlioz and Chopin also had a significant influence on his style. All three had in common an admiration for Italian *bel canto.* The essential Liszt, however, emerges when we look on him as the pupil of Czerny; as the youth who in Paris discovered for himself and for the public the works of Beethoven and Weber; as the editor and transcriber of Schubert, whose friend, Schober, was for a time Liszt's secretary, providing him with material for an (unwritten) Schubert biography; and as the elder musical brother of Richard Wagner. Add to this the Saint-Simonian and philanthropist; the kindest and most incorruptible of colleagues; the world-weary Catholic, as well as the man of the world who, even in his old age, was not averse to the adulation of ladies from all circles, particularly the highest – and the picture is rounded off in human, all too human, dimensions. Images such as 'Abbé Liszt at the Villa d'Este, thundering through the Waltz from Gounod's *Faust* while his cassock flutters about him' have circulated long enough. Our critical faculty should guard itself against anecdotes. In the Faustian seriousness of the B minor Sonata there is no room for ambiguities. One has to take Liszt seriously in order to play him well.

III

It is a peculiarity of Liszt's music that it faithfully and fatally mirrors the character of its interpreter. When his works give the impression of being hollow, superficial and pretentious, the fault lies usually with the performer, occasionally with the (prejudiced) listener, and only very rarely with Liszt himself.

Liszt's piano music depends to a great extent on an art that makes us forget the physical side of piano-playing. Yet it tends to be a vehicle for players of mere manual ability who lack any deeper musical insight. (In places where Liszt is viewed with disfavour, the conservatory students give themselves over with the same blind zeal to the demolition of Prokofiev sonatas.) The spell of 'technique for its own sake' will soon kill off the weaker brethren, and in the end it may well be Liszt himself who gets the blame for the whole epidemic.

In reality, Liszt stood in angry opposition to the drawing-room virtuosity of his time. He was first and foremost a phenomenon of expressiveness – Schumann called him 'Genie des Vortrags' ('a genius of interpretation') – so much so that he is said to have infused even Czerny and Cramer studies with radiant life. The frenzy and poetry of his music-making, allied to the new-found daredevilry of his technique, must not only have amazed the general public, but also dumbfounded his fellow pianists in the early years. Clara Wieck wrote to Robert Schumann, describing how Liszt's recitals had affected her: 'My own playing seems so boring and haphazard to me now – I've almost lost the inclination to go on tour again. After hearing and seeing Liszt's bravura, I feel like a student.' And again: 'Sometimes you think it's a spirit sitting there at the piano.' Technique served Liszt as a means of opening up new realms of expression. Anyone who is of the opinion that there is even one work by Liszt where gymnastics is the principal aim, had better keep his hands off this composer.

IV

A word about Liszt's form. One must not expect perfection in the Classical sense. The sonatas of Schubert, when measured by the yardstick of Classical form, already reveal nothing but flaws and shortcomings. There is something fragmentary about Liszt's work; its musical argument, perhaps by its nature, is often not brought to a conclusion. But is the fragment not the purest, the most legitimate form of Romanticism? When Utopia becomes the primary goal, when the attempt is made to contain the illimitable, then form will have to remain 'open' in order that the illimitable may enter. It is the business of the interpreter to show us how a general pause may connect rather than separate two paragraphs, how a transition may mysteriously transform the musical argument. This is a magical art. By some process incomprehensible to the intellect, organic unity becomes established, the 'open form' reaches its conclusion in the infinite.

Anyone who does not know the allure of the fragmentary will remain a stranger to much of Liszt's music, and perhaps to Romanticism in general.

V

This music, therefore, in no way 'plays itself'. One has to interpret it, and interpret it intelligently. Often it is only one step from the sublime to the ridiculous.

The pianist should be careful not to take that step. It is up to him whether pathos turns into bathos, whether Liszt's heroic fire freezes into a heroic pose, whether his rapt lyricism is smothered under perfumed affectation. He should give the passages of religious meditation simplicity, bring out the devilry behind the capriciousness, and convey the profound resignation behind the strangely bleak experiments of his late works.

He should be sure to use the original editions or the Breitkopf & Härtel Collected Works, and consult the *Liszt Pädagogium* (also published by Breitkopf & Härtel), a collection of notes made by some of Liszt's pupils about their studies with the master. Almost every other available publication is unreliable, with the possible exception of Sauer's reverent edition. Special attention should be paid to Liszt's pedalling instructions. They provide important information about declamation, colour and atmosphere; they create pedal points, underline harmonic connections. They should be observed, not literally, but in the spirit in which they were conceived: that way, the pedalling will not drown the music, but will let it breathe. The pianist should beware of dismissing out of hand pedal marks that seem to endanger clarity where there are numerous secondary notes. It is his job to create transparent textures with the aid of minute pedal vibrations. (Wilhelm Kempff's masterly Decca recordings are a perfect illustration of how this can be done.) Anyone who misconstrues the cadenzas at the start of *Totentanz,* with their chaotic agglomerations of tone masses, and insists on rattling them off *secco,* had better play Stravinsky.

Speeds should be kept in check – as far as the performer's bound-

less exuberance will permit! It has become virtually obligatory to play
Liszt as if he knew only one tempo indication: *prestissimo possibile*.
The poor E flat major Concerto in particular has become the target of
sporting ambitions. What is the present record – 14 minutes' playing
time? Or has it been bettered to 13? The performing style of the
mature Liszt tended rather towards majestic breadth; this is borne
out, in spite of all necessary scepticism about metronome figures, by
the tempo indications in Siloti's edition of *Totentanz* and in the *Liszt
Pädagogium.* As a conductor of Beethoven symphonies too, Liszt is
said to have taken slower tempi than was usual – 'with surprising
advantage to the overall effect', as even a conservative Leipzig
journal could not help but recognize.

Another danger to be avoided is excessive rubato. Of course, it is as
unwise to insist on strictness of tempo as it is to lapse into anarchical
freedom. Rhythm should be firm yet without constraint, masculine as
well as elastic. It should be remembered that Liszt transcribed the
First Mephisto Waltz and other piano pieces for large orchestra, so
the player should restrict himself in general to tempo modifications
that could be achieved by a first-rate orchestra under a first-rate
conductor. Liszt's music asks for refinement without pettiness.
Works like the Sonata and the Piano Concertos are not patchworks,
but symphonic organisms.

Liszt was one of the most amazing revolutionaries in the history of
music, and the pianist should prove this both to himself and to others.
He should present Liszt's daring harmony with such freshness as to
make the listener forget that new harmonic thresholds have been
crossed in the intervening hundred years. How 'modern' his late
compositions seem! It is no accident that the great pioneers Busoni
and Bartók vigorously defended his music.

We are all of Liszt's line. He created the type we aspire to: that of
the universal performer of grand stature. To him also we owe our
aural imagination and our technique. It would be nice if some of my
fellow pianists were to acknowledge this. It would be nice if the public
were to shed a few prejudices. A rehabilitation of Liszt is overdue.

(1961)

LISZT AND THE PIANO CIRCUS
– AN AFTERTHOUGHT

The denigration of Liszt has long since passed its peak. Today one almost has to defend him from those admirers who tend to see the whole nineteenth century as a kind of pianists' circus and would gladly subscribe funds for research into the achievements of Friedrich Kalkbrenner.

Yet the extent to which the circus is reflected in concert-giving should not be underestimated. The interpreter puts himself on display: a juggler, tightrope-walker and trapeze-artist of piano-playing, he performs tricks which even the supremely assured amateur would not believe himself capable of, and although he is not literally risking his neck, he does hazard his prestige for effortless security. It is this security of smoothly working reflexes rather than the communication of musical essentials which even today draws many deeply serious listeners to the concert hall, unaware of their motivation.

The engraving on the title page of Liszt's paraphrase of Halévy's *La Juive* (see plate facing p. 92) provides visible evidence of the fact that Liszt himself has contributed to the pianistic spectacular. Of course, his mastery of the instrument practically knew no bounds. But what musical daring underlies the pyrotechnics! How far removed Liszt's display is from the antics of the musical lightweights of his century whose bravura concertos have become the recent passion of a limited group of specialists! And, leaving the circus arena behind, how naturally did Liszt's music react to the Swiss countryside, to Italian works of art, or to the deaths of Hungarian friends! While it is being debated whether Henselt, Scharwenka or Moszkowski is to be preferred, even the best works of Smetana – whose Polkas hold a similar place in the music of his native country to that of Chopin's Mazurkas and Polonaises in Polish music – still remain virtually unknown.

That some of Liszt's own major piano works have fared no better is exemplified by the total neglect of his Variations on 'Weinen, Klagen, Sorgen, Zagen'. To me this is one of his most moving masterpieces. The stature of his original piano version – so vastly superior to the subsequent version for organ – is emphasized by the dedication to Anton Rubinstein, the century's other pianistic genius. Young pianists who played the work for Liszt in his last years were ironically informed by the master that 'this piece is a total flop'; how could anyone play such sombre 'hospital music' when art was supposed to be cheerful? The variations are in fact a passacaglia, leading into a fantasy on its chromatic ground bass and concluded by a chorale. The ground bass, identical with the bass line of the Crucifixus in Bach's B minor Mass, had also been used in Bach's Cantata *Weinen, Klagen, Sorgen, Zagen sind der Christen Tränenbrot.* Stirred by the psychological implications of this title, Liszt produced a superb example of programme music at its most emotional, and least pictorial. A very wide range of human suffering is suggested with almost austere concentration. Chromaticism stands for suffering and insecurity, while 'pure' diatonic harmony, introduced at the conclusion of the piece, represents the certainty of faith. We are reminded of the opening of Haydn's *Creation*, where Chaos and Light follow one another in a comparable way. In Liszt's work 'Light' is identical with the chorale 'Was Gott tut, das ist wohlgetan', which, incidentally, also closes Bach's Cantata. Liszt succeeds in offering relief without a trace of triviality: the entry of the chorale is a miracle of tenderness.

Liszt does not appear as the most self-critical of composers. Yet he realized sooner than anyone where the development of musical harmony would lead, and he adhered to this perception with admirable integrity. Consequently, his later pieces leave tonality, and consolation, behind. The analogy between religious faith and the faith in the imperishable power of the triad had ceased to ring true.

(1976)

LISZT'S HUNGARIAN RHAPSODIES

Two principal ways of approach have helped to make Liszt, or at least parts of his personality, more accessible to the modern listener. The first proceeds from new music, seeking in Liszt those elements which pointed towards the future – his drive towards experimentation, his revolutionary achievements that directly paved the way for the disintegration of tonality. The other path leads to Liszt's poetic-religious Romanticism, thus running the risk of giving preference to the Franciscan at the expense of the Gipsy.

This brings us to the Hungarian Rhapsodies. These are the pieces we perhaps have the most to make restitution to. One must defend them on two fronts: firstly, against musicians of the 'serious' breed who look down on them as showpieces, and secondly, against the piano maniacs who abuse them as showpieces. One must also contend with recollections of salon orchestras and bar pianists. Where is the masterpiece that is able to survive a bar pianist? It is above all the Rhapsodies that come to life through the improvisatory spirit and fire of the interpreter; they are wax in his hand like few other pieces in existence.

Not only Liszt, the Hungarian, was fascinated and inspired by the tunes from neighbouring Hungary, but also Brahms (and Haydn and Schubert before them). Liszt and Brahms even had an 'informant' in common, the violinist Reményi. There is still some confusion about the term 'Hungarian music'. It is not an entirely simple matter to draw a clear dividing line between three areas: that of the gipsy musical style, that of the folk melodies of the eighteenth and nineteenth centuries, which derived for the most part from the aristocracy and the middle class, and that of the actual folklore that was first brought to light through the research work of Bartók and Kodály. What the nineteenth century knew as Hungarian music seems to have been principally a conglomeration of gipsy style and 'urban' folk music. The gipsies helped themselves to the melodies of an Elemér Szentirmay or a Kéler-Béla and assimilated them into their style of performance, a style which aimed at the spontaneous and improvisatory. In that respect, gipsy music-making is related to jazz – which, incidentally, has exercised for some time a stimulating influence from its position on the fringe of 'art music', an influence similar to that exercised by 'gipsy music' a century earlier. Liszt made the mistake of crediting the gipsies for Hungarian national music; Hungary did not forgive him that for a very long time. Bartók and Kodály rectified the error, but in doing so they possibly went a little too far; they stigmatized the gipsies as mere imitators of a general Hungarian style, without granting them any creative identity whatever. All the same, the so-called gipsy scale (minor scale with altered fourth and major scale with altered second and sixth, respectively) was probably brought by the gipsies to Hungary from the Orient. In Hungarian folk music of the nineteenth century, however, it plays a lesser role than in Liszt's later works.

Strictly speaking, then, Liszt's Hungarian Rhapsodies belong to his paraphrases. Like Brahms in his Hungarian Dances, Liszt made use of 'urban' folk music melodies; standing quite apart from the phenomenal peasant folklore of Hungary, they have retained a freshness and charm in their own right. As to their working-out by Liszt, I quote Bartók, who did not care for the 'material' used, but who was forced to admit that 'the Rhapsodies, especially the Hungarian ones, are perfect creations of their own kind. The material Liszt uses in them could not have been treated with more genius and beauty.' This treatment takes possession of the principles of the gipsy style and heightens them to an infinite degree: the roving freedom, the romantic exaltation, the curious modulations, the volatility and abruptness, the renunciation of metrical fetters – all these elements were bound to awaken feelings of congeniality in Liszt. A multiplicity of pungent, darkly glowing and delicately languishing shades of tone colouration awaits rediscovery in the Hungarian Rhapsodies, in addition to characteristics that the public at the turn of the century can hardly have appreciated and possibly did not even notice: the Mephistophelian humour, the inclination to grotesqueness, the readiness to indulge in irony, mocking one's own intoxication. These characteristics should open up another route of access to Liszt for the modern listener.

Not all of the Rhapsodies contrast *lassú* (slow) with *friss* (fast), as does the famous, indestructible Second. The Eighth and Thirteenth, for example, combine the three basic characters of this kind of music: a defiantly or melancholically declamatory introduction, a coquettishly frisky Allegretto, and a fiery, whirling Presto. The delightful Thirteenth begins, incidentally, with a theme of somewhat Hebrew strain and develops from the Allegretto a marvellous climax in the style of Bellini. In the Third Rhapsody the *Friska* is lacking; the work is limited to the first two characters, which as B flat minor (close up) and G minor (far away) contrast poetically with one another. The sound of the cimbalom can be heard in the G minor episode, as in the beginning of the Eleventh. The Fifteenth Rhapsody is one of Liszt's three versions of the Rákóczy March, which Liszt first introduced to Berlioz.

Chopin paid musical tribute to his native country in a very different way from Liszt. While Liszt toys with chance, Chopin, in his Polonaises and Mazurkas, builds organisms. About the *Polonaise-Fantaisie*, one of Chopin's finest and most elusive works, Liszt made the following comments in 1851: 'An elegiac sadness dominates, interrupted by confused gestures. Melancholy smiles, unexpected tremors, awe-inspiring silences suggest the emotions of someone caught in a trap, enclosed from all sides.' Liszt speaks of 'despair which puts the mind into a state of near-delirious sensitivity', of 'groaning cramps of agony', and concludes that these are 'images of little convenience to art . . . . lamentable aspects which should be granted access to the territory of artistic production only with the utmost reluctance'. These lines may, of course, be inspired or even written by the Princess Sayn-Wittgenstein. Yet it seems surprising that a man who was to become so openly involved with the blackest sides of Romanticism in his own late compositions, would lend his name to such views.

The last four of the nineteen Hungarian Rhapsodies, along with pieces like *La lugubre gondola* (in two versions), *Unstern* ('Disaster'), the *Csárdás obstiné* and the *Csárdás macabre,* exemplify this trait. In his own words, Liszt's late music is to his earlier music as *l'amertume de cœur* is to *l'exubérance de cœur* (as bitterness of heart is to exuberance of heart). During his lifetime, Liszt's late compositions must have been considered the senile products of an old man, in so far as they were known at all. Tonality is undermined, the harmonic consequences of the gipsy scale are drawn. The sonorities become bleak and dwindle until only that which is indispensable remains, and sometimes less. Often, only the skeleton – not to say the ghost – of a piece is left. *Ostinato* figures heighten the torment of the monotony. Understanding for these death sighs and *danses macabres* has been found only in our time, a time which has become more accustomed to seeing the macabre with open eyes.

(1968)

LISZT'S PIANO-PLAYING

I

'Liszt: or the school of running – after women.'[1] This spiteful quip of Nietzsche's compresses popular prejudices into a single phrase. As so often with derogatory remarks, the essential point is ignored while the trivial is highlighted. The physical and profane aspects of Liszt's nature are concentrated on, to the exclusion of everything else. One senses the envy behind the calumny: envy of a good-looking man attractive to women, envy of a pianist endowed with a degree of technical facility and bravura that put his colleagues to shame. Two things, 'lusting after women' and Czerny's *School of Velocity* – a thoroughly arid collection of studies – are brought together in an association that might be witty if it were at all relevant to Liszt. It is a moot point whether in his relations with women Liszt was the pursuer rather than the pursued. To identify Liszt the virtuoso with the *School of Velocity*, however, is downright slander.

Robert Schumann, in a letter to Clara, said of Liszt: 'He is quite extraordinary. He played from the Novelettes, the Fantasy, the Sonata, moving me deeply. Many things were different from the way I had imagined them, but this was playing of genius, with a tenderness and boldness of emotion which I doubt if even he can summon up every day.' He went on: 'If you had been here this morning, I wager tears would have sprung to your eyes.' And Clara wrote to

---

[1] *Translator's note:* In an aphorism entitled *Meine Unmöglichkeiten* ('My Impossibles'), Nietzsche refers to 'Liszt: oder die Schule der Geläufigkeit – nach Weibern'. This is based on a pun on the words *geläufig* ('fluent') – as in Czerny's *Schule der Geläufigkeit* ('School of Velocity') – and *läufig* ('ruttish').

Schumann: 'When I heard Liszt for the first time in Vienna, I just couldn't control myself, I sobbed freely with emotion.' It is a testimony of Schumann's admiration for Liszt that he dedicated to him one of his most beautiful works, the Fantasy, Op. 17. Liszt reciprocated with his greatest creation, the B minor Sonata.

The relationship between Liszt and Brahms is sometimes misinterpreted. It is true that they had no great love for each other, but there is evidence of their mutual esteem. The story that Brahms dozed off during his visit to Weimar while Liszt was playing the B minor Sonata is unauthenticated, and not rendered any the more likely by the fact that Liszt bade Brahms a cordial farewell, presenting him with a silver cigarette case. Later on, the two met several times in Leipzig. Brahms sent Liszt his B flat major Concerto as soon as it had appeared in print, and Liszt acknowledged its receipt in a letter of reserved appreciation; nevertheless, he called it a masterpiece. When he listened to it in his class at Weimar in 1885 he praised it as 'one of Brahms's very best works'. (The diaries of Liszt's Austrian pupil August Göllerich show that between the years 1884 and 1886 works by Brahms were played for Liszt on several occasions in Weimar, Rome or Budapest. Liszt amused his class by inventing a nickname for one of the Paganini Variations: 'a rustle of cockchafers'.)

Even Eduard Hanslick, the feared Vienna critic and unrelenting opponent of the music of Liszt and Wagner, never ceased to respect Liszt as a man and as the outstanding pianist of his time. He held so high an opinion of Liszt that, before publishing his treatise *Vom musikalisch Schönen* ('The Beautiful in Music'), he invited him to write a preface for it – which Liszt, however, declined to do.

II

Liszt seems to have said little about technique to his pupils. It was taken for granted that anyone playing to him at Weimar would have the requisite mechanical abilities. When this proved not to be the case, Liszt would have one of his rare outbursts of rage – or else his 'Cerberus', Bülow, would feel obliged to bring his sarcasm into action: to a lady attempting to play Liszt's *Mazeppa* he once remarked, 'The only qualification you have for playing this piece is your horsiness.'[1]

---

[1] *Translator's note:* This quip, which alludes to the famous ride of Mazeppa, cannot be roundly translated. *Rossnatur* means 'a horse's nature', but also 'brute strength and patience'.

Liszt's teaching concentrated on interpretation. There certainly do not seem to have been many pianists who measured up to his ideal of technique; what he demanded was 'a technique created by the spirit, not derived from the mechanism of the piano'. 'All these', he explained ironically, pointing at his pupils when an old lady came to listen to one of his classes, 'are "pianists". At any rate, they all "play the piano"!' He had himself, however, mastered as a youth the whole range of studies and exercises so thoroughly that he could still play them as an old man. In later years he often complained that thumping and pounding was now the order of the day – a view shared by Clara Schumann, who, however, held Liszt responsible for this. Although there were many among his pupils who assiduously copied his hair style, there were few, apparently, who inherited any trace of his *cantabile* treatment of the keyboard. 'Everybody else', wrote Amy Fay about the grace of Liszt's piano-playing, 'sounds heavy beside him!' This American woman, who has given us an exceptionally lively description of Liszt, relates that she once asked him whether Sophie Menter, a rising star to whom Liszt had given strong support, was his pupil. 'He said no, he could not take the credit of her artistic success to himself.' Liszt did not consider himself a piano teacher.

III

In pictures and photographs showing Liszt at the piano we see him sitting relatively high and so far away from the instrument that his arms are almost straight. In moments of great elation he is said to have leant backwards. It is reported that he did not favour a strongly bent elbow position.

From the evidence of his works it is clear that the finger technique in general use up to that time was inadequate to his purposes. Nor can the new Deppe method of 'free fall' have satisfied him, since an unchecked arm drop onto the keys usually coarsens the sound. Only a balanced combination of muscle tone and relaxation is of value to the player.

Caricatures used to show Liszt in theatrical poses, with flailing arms and a fierce or ecstatic look in his eyes. In reality, at least in his later years, he did not care for exaggerated arm movements or for throwing his hands up in the air. ('Don't make an omelette!' he told a girl who would not keep her hands still.) This new restraint may explain the curious remark by Stradal, who studied with the master after 1880, that Liszt's entire technique, besides the finger technique, was a wrist technique. But what the great virtuoso, Arthur Friedheim, tells us is surely more to the point: that Liszt was to the end without equal in the production of powerful sound and towering dynamic climaxes. Such things are not done with the little finger.

(1976)

TURNING THE PIANO INTO AN ORCHESTRA (LISZT'S TRANSCRIPTIONS AND PARAPHRASES)

I

Among Liszt's works, there is a surprisingly large number of transcriptions – surprising to us of this century because we prefer to encounter a composer's works in their original form. Why did Liszt spend so much time and effort recomposing other people's music? (Did you read 'decomposing'? – Let us not prejudge the issue!)

Progress had been made in piano building. The range of colour and dynamics obtainable on a concert grand increased continually, along with the instrument's mechanical strength. The pianist discovered the piano anew – as the instrument capable of any transformation – and he discovered himself as the person capable of working those transformations. He could transform his piano into an organ, an oboe, an orchestra; himself into a conductor, a Lieder singer, a prima donna, into a chorus or speaking chorus (as in Liszt's *Pensées des Morts*), into a story-teller, gipsy, priest, dervish, or painter, into birds or the waves of the sea, even into the elements themselves. Alone, the protean player rules over the music, dependent on no one for help, and beholden to no one. In this spirit, Liszt played sections of Beethoven's *Pastoral* Symphony during an orchestral concert; we can be sure that his performance surpassed the prevailing standard of orchestral playing. In addition, he would vie with the great singers, bringing new music to the attention of the public at the same time. Thus, in an age before music was widely disseminated by the radio and the gramophone, Schubert, Wagner or Verdi reached a wide

REMINISCENCES

DE LA JUIVE

FANTAISIE BRILLANTE

Pour Piano seul

composée et dédiée

à Mslle Clémence Kautz

par

F. LISZT.

Leipzig, chez Fred. Hofmeister.

Pr. 1 Thlr.

The title page of Liszt's paraphrase of Halévy's *La Juive* (see p. 82).

Illustrations– & Photopress A.G., Zürich

Edwin Fischer

audience. Their music was impressed on a public held in thrall by the hypnotic or mesmeric power of the great virtuoso.

Transcribing can become an addiction. Many virtuosi of the last century succumbed to it, including some who, unlike Liszt and Busoni, lacked the credentials of being composers in their own right. Every edition of older music, with the exception of those by editors like Bischoff and Kullak, was virtually a transcription. Bülow 'corrected' Beethoven. Adolf Ruthardt, with no qualifications as composer, virtuoso or musical thinker, turned every masterpiece he touched into an Augean stable. Nor were contemporary pieces safe from 'embellishments', even those that could scarcely be said to have suffered from any lack of pianistic strength: Liszt's Second Legend of St Francis was inflated by his disrespectful pupil Stavenhagen in such a manner that the original looks by comparison like a simplified version for beginners. Of Liszt himself it was said that in his young days his rendering of other composers' music was best when he was sight-reading, since at that stage he was not yet able to add anything. And Busoni, during his late Berlin years, reportedly arranged passages from *The Merry Widow* in tenths while practising.

II

Are transcriptions, then, vindictive acts against helpless composers, springing from the transcriber's sense of his own inferiority? Hardly in the case of Liszt. Perhaps his pleasure in transcribing and paraphrasing can be partially explained by the fact that his orchestral works are of lesser stature than his best piano music. Not only was his grasp of larger forms insecure, but the actual scoring proved suitable mainly for the depiction of the crass, as in *Totentanz*. It was greatly surpassed by the subtlety and variety of his 'orchestration' on the piano. Chopin, though no transcriber at all, comes to my mind as a parallel case: with all his admiration for the great singers of his time, with all his ability to draw forth the loveliest cantilenas from the piano, he seemed incapable of putting together a really singable song.

Liszt's transcriptions can be classified as follows:

1) The literal transcriptions, where Liszt makes organ or orchestral works playable on the piano. Here belong his Bach transcriptions, and the piano reductions of the Beethoven symphonies, the Weber overtures, the *Symphonie Fantastique*, and the overture to Wagner's

Tannhäuser. (Anyone playing these pieces today will do well to refer back to the originals. He should not hesitate to rearrange the arrangement if this reflects the original better. For example, the climax of *Isoldes Liebestod* in Liszt's otherwise excellent transcription demands another solution than his crude chord vibrato.)

2) The operatic paraphrases, which are fantasies based on a single number or scene, or on several numbers, forming a cross-section of the opera *(Norma, La Juive, Don Giovanni).*

3) The song transcriptions, which range from relatively respectful arrangements to ruthless adaptations where cadenzas are interpolated, strophic repeats given a new illumination, and recapitulations climactically enhanced.

4) At least some of the Hungarian Rhapsodies, in which material taken from 'urban' folk music is paraphrased in a style that is derived from the mercurial performing habits of the gipsies, and from the sound of their instruments.

III

Liszt's transcriptions still form a unique exercise in 'orchestral' playing for the modern pianist. While in many other piano works the player has to uncover latent orchestral colours, here we have precise originals by which the results may be measured.

In endeavouring to produce orchestral colours on the piano, our concern must not only be with the timbre of each individual instrument, but also with the *manner* in which it is played – with certain peculiarities that arise from the construction of the instrument and that are reflected in the technique required by it. Another consideration is the number of players employed in a certain context. An orchestral *tutti* will have to be treated differently from a passage for strings alone; a *forte* for strings will need more volume than one for woodwind. For orchestral playing it is necessary to have a first-rate grand, voiced not too softly, in a room that is acoustically not too dry. The instrument should have metallic reserves at *fortissimo* level; its sordino pedal, however, should be free of metallic noises, and be capable of veiling the sound without making it thin and acid.

IV

How does one reproduce the timbre of other instruments on the piano? Perhaps the following hints will be useful.

Characteristic of the string sound is a wide, easily variable dynamic range, a legato supported by pedal vibrations, a tender onset of the notes, the moulding of single notes with the aid of accompanying figures, or simply by the power of suggestion. (If you believe that swelling on a note is not feasible for the pianist, you should have heard Edwin Fischer in the concert hall, playing the first entry in the Adagio of Beethoven's *Emperor* Concerto!) Bass entries may be anticipated. Cellos and double basses need time in which to unfold their sound. Pizzicato chords may be lightly broken; they are plucked away from the keys. Muted string passages of course require soft-pedalling.

In his 'string playing', the pianist ought to be familiar with the various kinds of bowing, in his 'wind playing' with the techniques of breathing. For the woodwind, there should be a distinct onset of the notes. The woodwind's clear articulation of each single note is best served by the avoidance, or at least a very careful application, of the pedal. The dynamic range should remain narrow.

The sound of the oboe I achieve with rounded, hooked-under and, as it were, bony fingers, in *poco legato*. The vibrato of the oboe requires some pedal, which, however, should not blur the progress from note to note. The pointed staccato of the oboe is pushed lightly into the keys. Dynamic range: *p* to *mp*.

The clarinet has the widest dynamic range – *pp* to *poco f*. Its sound is 'straight': *sempre poco tenuto* and *quasi senza pedale*. The normal sound of the B flat or A clarinets is a noble *mezzoforte* of dark, slightly veiled timbre, calling for the sordino pedal (and flexible wrists). The C and E flat clarinets, on the other hand, are unlyrical, shrill, grotesque; I play them with firm, 'hard' fingers.

The flute stays in *piano*; its dynamics are hardly apparent. Its timbre remains round, mild, somewhat colourless and veiled (I use the sordino, as long as it does not produce a thin or sharp sound). Whenever possible, I play every note with the help of a separate arm movement. The staccato should not be too well defined. Low notes on the flute should sound pale.

The cor anglais, whose characteristic *Tristan* sound is echoed in Liszt's *La lugubre gondola,* should be treated like a contralto voice with a very clear onset. The bassoon, on the other hand, remains usually without vibrato; it is rarely a cantabile instrument, and needs the sordino, but not the sustaining pedal. The touch is finger-staccato, the dynamic range *mp* to *mf*. Similar treatment is needed to achieve the grating sound of the bass clarinet and the double bassoon (dynamics: *mf*).

The noble, full, somewhat veiled, 'romantic' sound of the horn demands a loose arm and a flexible wrist. Although its dynamics extend from *pp* to *f*, the sordino pedal should always be used. In legato, every note is put down separately and connected with its neighbours by pedal alone. The staccato is never pointed. In chords played by several horns, the upper voice must recede slightly in favour of the lower ones.

A stiffening of the physical apparatus is required to do justice to the blaring, braying sound of the trumpet, the brilliance of which needs the aid of pedal. Dynamics: *poco f* to *fff*.

Trombones should be handled like horns, but without the sordino pedal. They produce the most opulent sound, and in piano writing usually appear as octaves. Brass chorales should be executed *portato*, with air between the chords.

Do not forget that the harp is a plucked instrument! The pianist should play harp notes with round, tensed fingers – *sempre poco staccato* – within the sustained pedal. In rapid, sharply ripped-off arpeggios, the finger-play is assisted by movements of the wrist. Harp figuration has a smooth outline; its dynamic curves are of geometrical precision. The rhythmic and dynamic spacing of the notes needs the utmost control. Harp arpeggios are the opposite of careless, chancy arpeggio playing. (Liszt's piano music is full of them, as for example in the recapitulation of the *Bénédiction*.) The dynamics of the harp range from *pp* to *mf*; several harps together can be stronger.

With the organ, a strict distinction must be made between the tone colour and strength of the manuals. Within each manual every part remains at the same level of volume. Declamation, therefore, is not produced by dynamics, but by articulation and the careful use of agogics (subtle inflections of rhythm). Arpeggios are excluded. Organ sound and church acoustics belong together, and the pianist has to reproduce that special resonance. This, along with pedal points and other long-sustained notes, creates fascinating pedalling problems, and here, above all else, lies the attraction of organ transcriptions. I try to manage with the right pedal alone, without using the

Steinway middle pedal. In Romantic organ music, the steady rise and fall of tone produced by the swell box will have to be imitated.

Organ transcriptions provide excellent training in colour control, in preparation for 'orchestral' playing.

V

My list of musical instruments would be gravely incomplete without the human voice. In its freedom of declamation it leaves the orchestra far behind. It is distinguished by warmth and directness. Its articulation is given shading by vowels and consonants, like sculpture in high relief. Its dynamics extend from whispering and humming to shouting. The voice is capable of every kind of expression. Vibrato, in all its degrees, characterizes singing; the arm of the pianist should sail on that vibrato like a ship on the water – a few centimetres above the keys. With the pedal assuring an unbroken legato, piano composers have often used the same finger for particularly 'singable' passages: the fifth in Schubert's G flat major Impromptu, the thumb in the third movement of Schumann's Fantasy, in his F sharp major Romanze, or in the second subject of Liszt's *Funérailles*. The sound produced in this way is more relaxed, more 'eloquent' than the *cantabile* of an actual finger-legato.

Singing means exhalation. But the moments of inhalation, too, can be musically significant, as will be felt by any player of song or opera transcriptions who is breathing with the vocal line. A sudden, gasping breath can make a strong dramatic effect – although not if it takes the form of an audible wheeze on the part of the pianist. Most of the time, however, a singer wishing to establish a coherent, large-scale view of the music will take breath as discreetly as possible: the musical ideal of the 'big breath', as we know, goes far beyond the physical limitations of breathing.

Piano literature is pervaded by the musical attitude of singing. Instruments like the organ and the harpsichord discouraged 'singableness'. The further the sound of the Hammerklavier departed from that of the harpsichord, the more accessible it became to cantilenas. Turning the piano into a vehicle of singing is not, to be sure, entirely Liszt's doing. But who else was able to make the *vox humana* vibrate so sensuously on the piano?

(1976)

FIDELITY TO LISZT'S LETTER?

I

The trust one can put in a composer's manuscript is a relative matter. The interpreter has to find out not only how the composer's notation is to be understood, but also how appropriate it is to each of his works. Not all masters have developed the same certainty and practical clarity of notation. With a composer like Beethoven, who notates the essential, expression marks and structural logic are often closely interrelated. It is a similar case with Brahms, who in this respect too had learnt from Beethoven. Utmost precision is found in Bartók; subtleness bordering on hypersensitivity in Reger and Berg; sparseness, mobilizing the player's adaptive faculties, in Busoni. *Cantabile* composers like Mozart and Schubert present the pianist with the task of translating vocal accents into their pianistic approximations. Schubert, moreover, shows himself to be a young composer lacking the experience that is gained from frequent performances.

Schumann too wrote his most outstanding piano works as a young man. His notation is a very personal mixture of pedantry and inexactness. He is pedantic in his insistence on minute variants by which, more often than not, he merely taxes the memory of the player without adding anything noticeably new to his recapitulations. He is inexact in his *ritardandi*, which at times are not succeeded by an *a tempo*. Two of his markings have often evoked smiles, one being *Durchwegs leise zu halten* ('To be kept soft throughout') over a movement – the third of the Fantasy, Op. 17 – which contains two fulminant dynamic climaxes, the other being *So schnell wie möglich* ('As fast as possible') in the G minor Sonata, which is followed in the coda by *Noch schneller* ('Still faster'). The first example is sheer nonsense. The second makes sense when the emphasis is shifted to 'As fast as *possible*', i.e. musically possible. The end of this movement will then become 'possible' at an even faster speed than the beginning.

The greatest riddle in musical notation is perhaps presented by Chopin. How can such sovereign mastery of the craft of composition go hand in hand with the clumsiness and irresolution shown in some of his manuscripts? I confess that I am not at all convinced by some of Chopin's markings. The liberty with which performers and editors have taken possession of Chopin's texts seems to me more understandable than in the case of other composers.

II

And what about Liszt? One can divide his works into two groups. The first comprises those compositions that are fully worked out, and where the text deserves to be followed precisely. (Here belong the B minor Sonata, the Legends, and the Variations on 'Weinen, Klagen, Sorgen, Zagen'.) The second group makes the intervention of the player possible or desirable.

This group is much larger. Liszt's manner of composing shows all the advantages and disadvantages of working at white heat. Almost always he produces fabulous, highly original beginnings – the tremendous rhetorical gestures in *Vallée d'Obermann*, the Dante Sonata, the *Malédiction*; the ecstasy, at first intangible, then materializing, a mirage become reality, in *Sposalizio* or the Petrarch Sonnet No. 123; the stagnant grief of *Pensées des Morts*; or the great expectations of the *Sursum corda* – which remain unfulfilled by the end.

For in Liszt's large-scale works, with the possible exception of the B minor Sonata, it is only very rarely that the expectations raised by the beginning are fulfilled. Disenchantment usually sets in during the last third of the piece. Instead of a structural development, which indeed could scarcely be worked out in the white heat of improvisation, Liszt offers a characteristic variant, or a series of repeats orchestrated ever more sumptuously or of ever-increasing excitement. *Mazeppa* rides four times, faster every time, to a contracting rhythm; *Sposalizio, Cantique d'amour* and the Dante Sonata are among the pieces where Liszt has indulged his whim of saying everything in triplicate. Sometimes one gains the impression that Liszt has lost interest in the shape of the whole: the A major Concerto and the Norma Fantasy in their printed editions even include suggested cuts *ad libitum*! Here, a composer born long before the development of aleatory methods reveals with disarming frankness his lack of confidence in pre-established and structured large-scale forms.

Another factor which might suggest the notion of 'coincidental form' in connection with Liszt is the number of *ossía* variants found in his piano music. Liszt's proposals for cuts are not prompted by any desire to tighten the argument; the works mentioned above are in any case of modest dimensions when compared with other Romantic piano concertos or with the sonatas of Schubert and Brahms. Just consider for a moment how odd authorized cuts would look in a movement by Schubert or Mahler, and you will realize how small a role the actual length of a piece plays in this matter. (Mendelssohn's conducting of the finale of Schubert's Great C major Symphony in a shortened version, and the pianist Harold Bauer's disfiguring cuts in his edition of the B flat major Sonata are based on misconceptions which are no longer prevalent.) Certainly, if one takes Bach, Mozart or Beethoven as the standard, one can speak of 'coincidental form' also in connection with Schubert and Mahler – a form that at times baffles the listener not only as to how, but also why a piece proceeds in the way it does. But this kind of coincidental form needs wide spaces in which to demonstrate that the usual order of things is here going to be called in question – or rather, from the standpoint of orderliness, to be deformed – and still we have not the slightest doubt about the validity of such a procedure. By comparison, Liszt's works – always excepting the B minor Sonata – seem to be built on doubts, perhaps in the hope that under the hands of a player of genius the suggestion of a new order will arise.

This reluctance to take a definite stand springs to some extent from the nature of the Romantic interpreter and improviser: he must convince the audience at the moment of performance that his, and no other, is the right way. (As a virtuoso, Liszt must have possessed this persuasive quality to the ultimate degree.) But the reverse side of the coin is Liszt's uncertainty in the composition of large-scale works. The grand view of the whole, which Beethoven held so securely, is often lost to him. It is only in the late works that this failing turns into a virtue: there, where there are no longer any apotheoses, where only emptiness, the dread of *senilità*, fixes its bold, bleak stare on us, the form gains from being open on all sides. Transitions occur here, after the example of late Schubert, in the shortest way, chromatically rising or falling, reduced to unison progressions. Endings dwindle over many lines, to trickle away in agony. Coincidental form has found its music.

III

Among the works of Liszt that invite or demand the intervention of the player are, first, the pieces in which there is a superfluity of notes. Most of these are from his virtuoso period. (Compare the third, more playable version of the Transcendental Studies with the overblown second.) Incidentally, there is also a superfluity of notes – not intrinsically so, but for playing purposes – in the B flat major Concerto of Brahms. It contains a number of double-stop passages, the part-writing of which is notated without regard for what is pianistically possible or even necessary. A pianist failing to adapt these passages puts himself at risk: he yields to a compulsion to deliver distinctly every printed note without enquiring into the meaning of the passage; he may impair that meaning if he is then forced, say in the notorious double thirds of the finale, to play at slower speed and in a cumbersome *mezzoforte* what should be fleet, scurrying and *pianissimo*; he underestimates the readiness of a gifted and cultivated ear to restore automatically certain inessential notes that have been sacrificed to the higher purpose – such an ear will not even be aware that those notes are missing, as long as the player does not make things unduly easy for himself.

Secondly, there are works which in places give the impression of a sketch, such as the extremely peculiar *Pensées des Morts* and a number of late pieces where, at the very least, the interpretative intentions of Liszt have to be divined, and where many a metronome mark deserves close scrutiny.

In the third place, there are those works which have induced individual players to tailor them to their technique. D'Albert and Busoni performed their own versions of the First Mephisto Waltz. However, it is a moot point whether the Mephisto Waltz or *La Campanella* are really in need of Busoni's slimming treatment. Liszt himself invented numerous new variants for many passages.

Finally, mention must be made of the *ad libitum* cadenzas, like the one in the Second Hungarian Rhapsody. (D'Albert, Rachmaninov and Cortot have furnished splendid interpolations.)

IV

In Liszt's works, as in those of other composers, there are wrong notes and accidentals that cling tenaciously to the music. On their respective recordings of the A major Concerto, the two Liszt pupils Sauer and Weingartner left uncorrected the wrong pizzicato bass E of the original print, which the Collected Edition had amended; the note must of course be G, as it leads to the A flat of the next piano bass (letter H of the score).

Liszt had a mania for harp-like sounds. While it would be better to avoid certain arpeggios, particularly when they occur in *forte* cantabile passages, it would be a grave mistake to condemn all breaking of chords. Busoni's slender, sculptured sound, Toscanini's tendency to 'detonate' accents, and Stravinsky's brittle clarity have left their mark on us, making us suspicious of soft contours. The abolition of the arpeggio ran parallel to the abolition of the portamento in singing and string playing. The result has been an impoverishment of music's means of expression. The breaking of chords is not necessarily a makeshift device for small hands, just as the slurring of sung notes is not necessarily a sign of bad taste. As a vehicle for the attainment of *cantabile* playing and a spatial, plastic sound quality, the arpeggio as well as the discreet, preparatory anticipation of the bass (and, more rarely, the pronounced anticipation of the melodic line) must have been indispensable to an age which, to a much higher degree than our own, strove towards the ideal of a beautiful, singing piano tone. Used automatically and excessively, however, these expressive devices lose their charm and defeat their own purpose, as can be observed from the records of Paderewski. Indiscriminate and tasteless use may well have been the main cause of the oblivion into which arpeggios and portamenti have fallen. Their rediscovery should be the concern of our more gifted pianists, singers and string players.

Liszt's pedal marks are, like all pedalling instructions, intended merely as suggestions – they have to be adapted to individual instruments and concert halls. Moreover, allowance must be made for the subtleties of minute pedal vibrations which cannot be notated. It is dangerous to ignore them: the three-dimensional character of Liszt's sound-imagination should not be flattened out. Even the long pedals in the exposition of the Dante Sonata or in the bass-octave passage of *Funérailles* prove their expressive power in certain acoustic conditions. Anyone substituting dry staccato gymnastics for the awesome, gradually increasing dynamic suction demanded here, misunderstands and falsifies Liszt.

Liszt's notation may often be incomplete. Any additions or modifications made by the player, however, must be undertaken in the spirit in which a modern pianist fills in the piano concertos of Mozart: that is, in the style of the composer. To modernize Liszt makes no sense. It is enough to discover him.

(1976)

BUSONI

A PECULIAR SERENITY
On the Thirtieth Anniversary of Busoni's Death, 1954

I

For most people ambiguity holds little attraction. They mistrust the contradictions they find in those who have learnt to keep a balance between the opposing forces of their personality. What they look out for is hardly something which will disturb them by enlarging their view of life, but something which will reassure them by simplifying it. Of many possible ideals, they demand that only one be established as absolute and disapprove of an attitude which concedes a certain degree of truth to each of those ideals in the belief that 'every error is a masked truth' – an attitude which, instead of reaching out to barren extremes, strives towards a consciously controlled synthesis.

Busoni, possessing just such an all-embracing spirit – 'a kind of musical Leonardo', as Wilhelm Kempff boldly called him – is virtually unrivalled in the history of music. He was a world-famous, phenomenal pianist, a conductor of new orchestral works, a composer of highly significant music for the stage and concert hall, the importance of which has not yet been appreciated; he was a theorist of genius, a highly cultured man of letters, a devotee of theatre as a sublimation of life, and of life as an extension of theatre; he was a world citizen, a child of his strife-torn age, and the prophet of a music of the future that was to be freed from the shackles of the 'law-givers'.

As a boy, Busoni effortlessly acquired pianistic skill. As a travelling prodigy, he was hailed enthusiastically by none other than Hanslick, the 'law-giver' *par excellence.* As a youth, he was encouraged in composition by Arrigo Boito. As a virtuoso of almost thirty, he made his first investigation of the works of Liszt, which brought about a striking transformation. After a creative pause of about ten years, Busoni had finally gained an artistic profile of his own; the easy routine which had kept his entire earlier production on the tracks of eclecticism had now been banished. The first works to show to the full his individual style as a composer are some of the Elegies of 1908, expressly designated 'Six new piano pieces'.

The master of the keyboard had long since left behind the 'pianistic Darwinism' of his contemporaries and, at the opposite spiritual pole to d'Albert, had taken the leading place in the Liszt succession. Without having been a personal pupil of Liszt, it was Busoni who was foremost in cultivating Liszt's spiritual heritage – by going beyond it. Through him, piano technique underwent its apparently ultimate differentiation. Lucid awareness cleared away the ruggedly demoniac and the accidental. It is significant that Bach and Liszt were the two nerve centres of Busoni's enormous repertoire: the basis and the apex of pianism. The contemplative inwardness of the one was as congenial to him as the theatrical and mysterious tone-magic of the other.

Busoni's allegiance to such dissimilar gods has often been misunderstood. Those unable to grasp the polarities of his nature have tended to brand him a Jack-of-all-trades trying to hide his lack of inner consistency behind a façade of fabricated originality. And indeed, on investigation of his talents, inclinations and pronouncements, the observer is faced with an image that is equivocal.

On the one hand, Busoni's Latin sense of form made him hate the chaotic. His idea of a 'Young Classicism' aimed to incorporate experimental features in 'firm, rounded forms', which, however, should be motivated each time by musical necessity and never simply yield to the pressure of traditional models. On the other hand, there was in him an overwhelming yearning for untrammelled, soaring music, leaving behind formal conventions, as manifested by the fantasies that precede baroque fugues and by certain free introductions and bridge passages. The consequence of this attitude is made apparent in the following statement from his *Entwurf einer neuen Ästhetik der Tonkunst* ('Outline of a new aesthetic of music'):

'In present-day musical practice the rest and the pause are the elements which reveal most clearly the origins of music. Great performers, improvisers, know well how to use these expressive tools on a larger scale. The spell-binding silence between two movements becomes, in this context, music itself. It leaves more room for mystery than the actual sound, which, by its higher degree of definition, permits less elasticity.'

On the one side, there was Busoni's passionate struggle with the problems of counterpoint, his untiring speculative quest which in 1911 produced the first polytonal fugue exposition and in the *Rondo Arlecchinesco* of 1916 led him to the use of a twelve-note theme; on the other, there was his statement that 'improvisation would come closest to the essential nature of art if only it were within man's power to master inspiration extempore'.

While Busoni demanded that creation should start from the non-existent, should search for the unknown, the never yet experienced, should forget all received ideas and look solely towards the future, at the same time he fostered the cultivation and utilization of the past, dreaming of a future art that would be aristocratic and reserved, reactionary in the noblest sense. Thus his fondness for the technique of transcription – of which more shall be said later – must also be seen as a characteristic attempt to combine the conservation of historical values with the powerful urge to innovate.

With Busoni, an exceptionally strong identification with the instrument was carried to the point of self-contradiction in such notions as 'abstract sound', the 'dematerialization' of music, the emancipation of musical instruments from their conventional applications, the concept of a 'de-individualization' of musical timbre.

In the same breath, he spoke of systems of philosophy and religion as artistic manifestations which would carry conviction according to the skill of their propagators, and, in a fit of religious fervour, called music 'the heavenly child whose feet touch not this earth'.

Again, there was the Faustian side of his intellect, which made him familiar with the melancholy of loneliness. As its counterbalance we find serene confidence, rarefied irony, and ready surrender to grace, that mysterious, ethereal virtue, rarest attribute of spirits.

How a character of such individuality was able to avoid those compulsive exertions of the will that often bring ruin to problematic natures, will for ever remain a mystery. The love of Mozart that took hold of Busoni in his late maturity is a signpost on the road of his inner development. 'In the most tragic situation, he is ready with a joke – in the most hilarious, he is capable of a learned frown' (*Mozart Aphorisms*, 1906). Paul Bekker in his funeral oration commented on the 'peculiar serenity' of Busoni the man, which raised him above others. In Busoni's best works, there is an effortless fusion of the Classicist and the Romanticist, the constructor and the improviser, the virtuoso and the transcendentalist of sound, the aesthete and the mystic, the magician and the comedian.

II

Since Liszt, pianistic progress has been made along many lines. We owe some new nuances to the Impressionists, the modern Russians and Bartók. But it was Busoni alone who realized the full implications of the instrument's technical possibilities over their whole range, beyond the achievements of specialists.

The most individual feature of Busoni's pianistic art was his treatment of the pedal. 'The effects of the pedal remain unexplored because its use is still fettered by a narrow-minded and unreasonable harmonic theory; people treat the pedal in much the same way as they might try to force air and water into geometric shapes . . . . The pedal has a bad reputation. Meaningless infringements of the rules bear the blame for this. Now let us try some meaning*ful* infringements . . . .' In conjunction with a highly refined non-legato technique this new treatment of the pedal produced tone colours and areas of sound of the most delicate transparency. It was particularly those passages in his piano works which to the uninformed seem technically overloaded that, according to Gisella Selden-Goth, became under Busoni's hands 'a disembodied, floating sound mixture, gliding and whirling past in iridescent shades'.

To Busoni, technical difficulties are merely coincidental. All that matters is the musical meaning of a difficult passage. Until one understands that meaning, one should not touch the keys. The pianist has one implacable enemy: the piano, which continually tempts him to forget the musical meaning of a passage in mastering its mechanical difficulties. Technique can never reach a point where problems cease to exist, precisely because the real problems are not technical, but musical. Liszt's notion of 'technique as the helpmate of the idea' finds a strong exponent in Busoni.

He never tired of protesting against the prejudice that saw in Liszt no more than the conceited acrobat and breaker of hearts. At present, the compositions of Busoni are suffering a similar fate to those of Liszt: they are written in an ink that, as it were, begins to glow only when the right eye falls upon it. But while the creations of Liszt are no longer known,[1] those of Busoni have yet to become known. I would recommend a thorough study of the *Fantasia Contrappuntistica,* that monumental fusion of thesis and antithesis, of counterpoint and fantasy, Bach and Busoni, that confrontation of an infinitely subtle range of keyboard colours with a Baroque-style independence from tone colour. The student of this work may find himself transported into a novel sphere of instrumental art.

III

Busoni's piano-playing signifies the victory of reflection over bravura. After Liszt had triumphantly brought the instrument out from its narrow isolation, Busoni continued the process to the point where its challenge seemed to have been overcome. However, pianistic impulses are never abolished; they are merely filtered and refined. In his own words: 'Have thunderstorms ceased to exist because Franklin invented the lightning conductor?' For Busoni, too, knew the favour of the hour. In a letter to his wife he describes the happy occasion: when the instrument responds perfectly, when the best ideas come during the actual performance and, what is more, sound right straight away . . . .

One cannot imagine an art of interpretation farther removed from mindless routine. On the subject of routine, flourishing not least at the conservatories (whose main purpose, according to Busoni, is to provide a livelihood for the teachers), Busoni had much to say from his own experience:

'Routine means the acquiring of a little experience and a few tricks of the trade, and the unvarying application of them to any given context. Accordingly, the number of related contexts must be remarkably high. To my mind, however, music is so constituted that every context is a new context and should be treated as an "exception". The solution of a problem, once found, cannot be reapplied to a different context. Our art is a theatre of surprise and invention, and of the seemingly unprepared. The spirit of music arises from the depths of our humanity and is returned to the high regions whence it has descended upon mankind . . . .'

Busoni has demonstrated the decisive importance of subjectivity in

[1] Since 1954, the situation has changed in many countries, as I have indicated earlier in the book.

interpretation, with all that entails; it is not, however, a subjectivity dictated by blind instinct, but one controlled by a sovereign intelligence. As Liszt put it, the work is for the interpreter the tragic and stirring *mise en scène* of his own emotions. A musical transcription, therefore, would be the result of the compromise between what the composer had to say and what the interpreter felt about it. Anyone doubting the propriety of such an artistic exercise should remind himself that the only point at issue is the persuasive power of the arranger. The age of virtuoso worship has been succeeded by one of ancestor veneration for the composer. But let us not forget that above the distinction between composer and performer there is the primal element of music itself to which both are subjected, that elemental power beyond human concerns from which the composer draws his inspiration and to which the true interpreter returns the creations of music. 'The interpretation of music springs from those sublime heights from which the art of music itself has descended. When music is in danger of becoming earthbound, the interpreter has to raise it up and guide it back to its original elevated state.'

A Utopian thought, certainly. But in Utopia art has both its source and its destination.

ARLECCHINO AND DOKTOR FAUST
On the Centenary of Busoni's Birth, 1966

A lady of the Busoni circle once asked me what it was about Busoni that so attracted us younger musicians – after all, none of us had been under the spell of his personality or had had direct experience of the magic of his piano-playing. None of us had encountered his supreme personal charm, the powerful, even paralysing presence of Busoni the man. Let me attempt to answer this question.

First, there was that quality that lifted Busoni out from the ruck of his contemporaries, the same quality that had distinguished Liszt fifty years before: the universality of his mind which transcended the confines of his pianistic renown. There was the breadth of his interests and learning; the impact he made on the people he met, enhanced as it was by his splendid appearance; his literary education and activity, besides his ability to correspond in four languages; the witty draughtsmanship of the caricaturist; the aura, at once awe-inspiring and ludicrously fantastic, which, we are told, surrounded him. To all these qualities must be added his achievements as a musician: the composer whose late-style works are to be counted among the most significant of his age; the virtuoso pianist who became a model to the succeeding generation in Europe, paralleled only by d'Albert, who in many other respects was his direct opposite; the conductor who gave first performances of new compositions; the teacher who in Weimar revived the great days of Liszt and in Berlin counted Wladimir Vogel, Weill and Jarnach among his composition students; and lastly the champion of modern music, in whose collection of essayistic and poeticizing fragments entitled *Entwurf einer neuen Ästhetik der Tonkunst* ('Outline of a new aesthetic of music') are foreshadowed not only dodecaphonic and microtone systems, but even electronic music – and that in the year 1906! Such, then, was Busoni's universality.

In the second place I should like to mention a characteristic pertaining to Busoni the pianist, something perhaps unique to him and to Liszt, namely the combination of the great musician and artist with the great bravura player whose strength and precision overcame all difficulties. It is, incidentally, not quite true that we have never heard Busoni play. At least, his recording of the Thirteenth Hungarian Rhapsody by Liszt proves that the admiration of Schnabel, Fischer, Kempff or Steuermann was justified.

My third point seems to me the most important: occupying ourselves with the late compositions of Busoni gives us pleasure. Fischer-Dieskau sings Doktor Faust and the Goethe songs; Hans Werner Henze champions the operas *Turandot* and *Arlecchino;* some pianists, endowed with the requisite large hands, attempt Busoni's Sonatinas and Elegies, the *Fantasia Contrappuntistica,* the Toccata and the organ transcriptions. However, there is a reserve peculiar to his best works which cuts them off from loud acclaim. To quote his biographer, E. J. Dent: 'He was Latin enough to avoid by nature the sentimentality of the second-rate Germans, and at the same time too German to fall into sentimentality of an Italian type.'

His German-Italian heritage is manifest in the titles of his two most important stage works, *Doktor Faust* and *Arlecchino.* In other respects too, these works tell us a great deal about Busoni. They show both the speculative and the playful elements in his nature. But they also represent the two possibilities in which Busoni, equally critical of Wagner and of the *Verismo,* saw the future of opera. These are the concepts of 'supernatural subject-matter' (*übernatürlicher Stoff*) and 'downright playfulness' (*absolutes Spiel*). His view that 'opera should create an illusory world which reflects life in either a magic mirror or a distorting mirror' is clearly borne out not only by the *Commedia dell'arte,* but also by the puppet play (*Doktor Faust,* Gozzi's *Turandot*) and the fantastic world of E. T. A. Hoffmann (*Die Brautwahl*).

Hoffmannesque traits are also to be found in Busoni's private life: it is reported that in the years before his death in 1924 he sought out the company of the deformed; yet at the same time he was striving for lucidity and lightness (Busoni's nature was activated by its contradictions). One aspect of this striving was his call for a 'Young Classicism', which had little to do with Neo-Classicism. As he wrote to Gisella

Selden-Goth: 'The tapering-scale [*Verjüngung*] – a technical architectural term – implies, as you know, a slimming, a refinement of lines. Therefore we should speak not of New Classicism (a term I resist, since it sounds like a turning back), but of Young Classicism [*Junge Klassizität*].'[1] Busoni was fond of paradoxical formulations, a characteristic he shared with his contemporary Oscar Wilde. One of his remarks that has come down to us by word of mouth, and which was coined with a certain Late-Romantic virtuoso in mind, runs 'Poetry in performance is a lack of technique.' Some Busoni disciples may well have taken too literal a view of this and similar strange pronouncements, such as his sharp criticism of early Beethoven in particular, his total disregard of Schubert, his low opinion of Schumann, his opposition to Wagner and Debussy. Against these things, however, should be measured Busoni's boundless admiration for Mozart ('With every riddle he gives you its solution'), his incomparable advocacy of Liszt, his sympathy with César Franck, Saint-Saëns, Alkan, his respect for Strauss, Mahler and Schoenberg (who succeeded him at the Berlin Hochschule), his interest in Stravinsky's *Histoire du Soldat.*

The transient nature of some of his views should not blind us to the value of Busoni's works. In Vienna – a city, according to Busoni, that is suffocated by its *feuilletons* – Busoni the composer has not yet been noticed. At most, he is known as the arranger of Bach who arouses the wrath of the purists, for in these days even masterly arrangements are deemed sacrilegious. Elsewhere, the slowly growing fame of Busoni the composer is based on post-war performances of his operas. *Doktor Faust,* in stage or concert versions, has been given in Berlin, London, Florence and New York. It remains to be seen how many more Busoni anniversaries must go by before one of the quintessential operas of the twentieth century finds its way to Vienna.

---

[1] *Translator's note:* As will be obvious to the reader, the English language cannot reproduce the play on the word *jung* ('young') that Busoni intended here.

AFTERTHOUGHTS ON BUSONI

I

The first of my essays on Busoni, the idiom of which strikes me today as odd, is permeated by Busoni's own individual use of language. It is full of Busoni quotations (by no means always confined within inverted commas), such as his label 'pianistic Darwinism'. In his essay *Das Klaviergenie* ('The Pianist of Genius') Busoni wrote: 'It is very surprising – at first sight, anyway – that something which until recently could be done only by one man should now also be done by another; but when there are hordes of "others", it becomes Darwinism.' Another Busonian expression, 'law-givers', denotes those to whom the signs are more important than the music. Commenting on Busoni's *Entwurf einer neuen Ästhetik der Tonkunst* ('Outline of a new aesthetic of music'), Arnold Schoenberg, who said of himself that he was 'certainly no law-giver, hardly even a law-taker', repudiated with splendid acuity the right of the interpreter to encroach upon the creator:

'The more an interpretation respects the written symbols, or rather, the more it tries to deduce from them the true intention of the author, the higher it must be rated. For the interpreter is not the tutor, let alone the spiritual mentor, of an orphaned work of art, but its keenest servant. His desire is to apprehend every wish that the composer utters, to cherish his every thought, scarcely conceived. But this ideal is marred by two imperfections: that of notation, and that of the servant himself. For, unfortunately, the servant is likely to be an individual bent on exhibiting his own personality rather than on inhabiting that of the composer. Thus he will usually become a parasite on the skin of the composer, when he could have been an artery in his bloodstream.'

Liszt's observation that 'the work is for the interpreter the tragic and stirring *mise en scène* of his own emotions' shows where Busoni's ideas came from. It also shows up the type of interpreter Schoenberg was alluding to – though this did not prevent him from calling Liszt a great man.

II

My own ideas about the task of the interpreter have moved away from those of Busoni. In my view, the interpreter should function in three capacities: as curator of a museum, as executor of a will, and as obstetrician. The job of the curator is an 'historical' one: he compares the text of the work with the original sources and familiarizes himself with the textual conventions and performing habits of the period. In doing so, he will discover that it is not enough to 'observe the letter' – as he will see if he should look, for example, at the Mozart piano concertos, the solo parts of which have hardly any dynamic markings, but contain fermatas and uncompleted passages that have to be filled in by the player. At this point the curator hands over to the executor, who realizes that it is his own breath which revives the breath of the composer, and who is aware that emotions and ears, instruments and concert halls have changed since the composer's day. The executor must not only have the ability to project the music of the past into the present, but also a faculty for reopening the gates of the past, for making what was new in its time seem new once again. Thus, for instance, he will reinvest the chord of the diminished seventh, which wore increasingly thin in the course of the nineteenth century, with its former ominous, demonic, tonality-denying tension whenever this is required by the music.

If fortune smiles, the 'moral' function of the executor will be complemented by the 'magical' function of the obstetrician. It is he who protects the performance from the cold touch of finality, who leads the music back to its origin: the work, so it seems, is brought to life by the hands of the player. The immediacy of such a feat renders pointless any discussion about the merits and demerits of tradition. From a carefully nurtured foundation springs spontaneity.

III

Some of Busoni's works have recently profited from the vogue for Victorian or Edwardian curiosities[1] and the rediscovery of Art Nouveau. But compositions like the monstrously overwritten Piano Concerto or the bravura pieces among the Elegies obstruct our view of his superlative late piano music. How topical still – and undiscovered – are the first two Sonatinas, the rest of the Elegies, and the Toccata of 1921! The erosion of the years has not smoothed over their unyielding surface. No patina of familiarity softens their sharpness. *Doktor Faust,* now as ever, towers over the musical theatre of its time, alongside the works of Berg, Schoenberg and Weill. No great conductor and producer have yet joined forces in a production of this work. Will there be a demand one day for the staging of *Doktor Faust* in its incomplete form, as has happened with *Moses und Aron* and *Lulu?* The final monologue, which remained uncomposed at Busoni's death, could be spoken. Busoni had been an uneven composer. But in a work where a new style reached its consummation, this new-found unity should not be broken up by foreign interpolations.

(1976)

---

[1] cf 'Liszt and the Piano Circus', p. 82.

EDWIN FISCHER

REMEMBERING MY TEACHER

Edwin Fischer was, on the concert platform, a short, leonine, resilient figure, whose every fibre seemed to vibrate with elemental musical power. Wildness and gentleness were never far from each other in his piano-playing, and demonic outbursts would magically give way to inner peace. It was as little trouble to him (as Alfred Polgar once said of an actor) to lose himself as to find himself. His playing of slow movements was full of an unselfconsciousness beside which the music-making of others, famous names included, seemed academic or insincere. With Fischer, one was in more immediate contact with the music: there was no curtain before his soul when he communicated with the audience. One other musician, Furtwängler, conveyed to the same degree this sensation of music not being played, but rather happening by itself. His death was a grievous blow to Fischer.

Just as Furtwängler liked to play the piano in his very personal manner, so Fischer loved to conduct. Here, too, his achievement was breathtaking. His way of directing the concertos of Bach, Mozart and Beethoven from the keyboard remains inimitable. Anyone in doubt should listen to his recording of the second movement of Bach's C major Concerto for Three Pianos: perfect unity reigns from the first note to the last.

However, Fischer should be remembered not only as a solo pianist and conductor, but also as a chamber musician, song accompanist and teacher. Fischer's ensemble with Mainardi and Kulenkampff – whose place was later taken by Schneiderhan – reached the heights of trio playing, and as a partner of Elisabeth Schwarzkopf the master achieved the ideal fusion of simplicity and refinement. As an inspiring teacher he led two generations of young pianists 'away from the piano, and to themselves', and provided them with proper standards for their future careers. As an editor he helped to restore the *Urtext* of Classical masterpieces, and as a writer he formulated such memorable precepts as 'Put life into the music without doing violence to it.' Can there be a simpler formula for the task of the interpreter?

All this calls to mind Alfred Cortot, as many-sided an artist as Fischer. The two masters, who had great admiration for each other, were poles apart in their repertoire; one could say that they complemented one another. Fischer was in his element in the Classic-Romantic realm of 'German' music, with Bach, Mozart, Beethoven, Schubert and Brahms. Cortot was particularly happy with Chopin, with some of Liszt's works, and with French piano music. In Schumann, their spheres met. At home, as he once told me, Fischer liked to play Chopin, whereas Cortot is reported to have had a sneaking affection for Brahms.

Fischer was anything but a perfect pianist in the academic sense. Nervousness and physical illness sometimes cast a shadow over his playing. But in the avoidance of false sentiment he was unrivalled. Moreover, as the initiated will know, it would be presumptuous to underrate a technique that made possible performances of such fabulous richness of expression. The principal carrier of this expressiveness was his marvellously full, floating tone, which retained its roundness even at climactic, explosive moments, and remained singing and sustained in the most unbelievable *pianissimo*. (In conversation, Fischer once compared piano tone to the sound of the vowels. He told me that in present-day musical practice the *a* and *o* are neglected in favour of the *e* and *i*. The glaring and shrill triumphs over the lofty and sonorous, technique over the sense of wonder. Are not *ah!* and *oh!* the sounds of wonder?) By bringing the middle parts to life, Fischer gave his chord-playing an inward radiance, and his *cantabile* fulfilled Beethoven's wish: 'From the heart – may it go to the heart.'

As a teacher, Fischer was electrifying by his mere presence. The playing of timid youths and placid girls would suddenly spring to life when he grasped them by the shoulder. A few conducting gestures, an encouraging word, could have the effect of lifting the pupil above himself. When Fischer outlined the structure of a whole movement, the gifted ones among the participants felt they were looking into the very heart of music. He sometimes helped us more by an anecdote or a comparison than would have been possible by 'factual' instruction.

He preferred demonstration to explanation; again and again he would sit down himself at the piano. Those were the greatest, the unforgettable impressions retained by his students. In the days before his prolonged illness, his vitality knew no bounds. He was happy to be surrounded by young people who trusted in him, and his playing for us was at its most beautiful. On such occasions, we experienced what he told us in these words: 'One day, the piano has all the colours of the orchestra; another day, it brings forth sounds that come from other worlds.'

(1960)

AFTERTHOUGHTS ON EDWIN FISCHER

I

What is piano-playing of genius? Playing which is at once correct and bold. Its correctness tells us: that is how it has to be. Its boldness presents us with a surprising and overwhelming realization: what we had thought impossible becomes true.

Correctness can be attained by the expert. But boldness presupposes the gift of projection, which draws the audience into the orbit of one's personality. The personal, 'impossible' element in Edwin Fischer was twofold: his playing sprang from a childlike nature, yet, if the signs were favourable, it also possessed all the wisdom of the experienced master. The childlike characteristics were his sincerity and spontaneity, his ready sense of wonder, constantly rediscovered, his joy in playing, clowning, daring – with what breathless gusto he sometimes romped through a Mozart Allegro! The master in Fischer was proclaimed by his gift for emotional differentiation, by the beauty of his tone and its extreme refinements, by his vision as well as by his grasp of the grand design. Child and master formed a perfect union in Fischer's happiest achievements; there was nothing to pull them apart.

II

Piano-playing is a strict discipline. Practice – the task of clarifying, purifying, fortifying and restoring musical continuity – can turn against the player. Control can 'sit' on one's playing like a coat of mail, like a corset, or like a well-tailored suit. On lucky occasions, it is just there, as if in league with chance. I have never come across a control of line and nuance more exciting than that achieved by Fischer in his performances of the slow movement of Bach's F minor Concerto, in the long paragraphs of the A minor Fantasia, or in some pieces from *The Well-Tempered Clavier.* (These examples should suffice to call to order the detractors of Fischer's technique!) Yet this excitement does not obstruct the listener – it liberates him. There is something untamed even about Fischer's most decorous playing. 'In the work of art,' says Novalis, the German Romanticist, 'chaos must shine through the adornment of order.' (*Im Kunstwerk muss das Chaos durch den Flor der Ordnung schimmern.*) Fischer's order does not betray the pressure of reason; it represents creation in a state of innocence. So, does control appear in the guise of improvisation, as with the great Cortot? I would rather say that Fischer completes a circle: setting out from improvisation, he takes the route of a finely regulated awareness which eventually leads him back to improvisation.

There are pianists whose playing is so predictable that if they fell into a faint it would create a welcome diversion. Fischer could spring a surprise at every note; he could also alarm you with his nerves, or make your hair stand on end with his childish fancies (as in his dreadful cadenzas!). There are pianists who hang on the music like parasites, and there are the platform hyenas who devour master-pieces like carrion. Fischer was a giver; he let out his breath and recommended his pupils to practise exhaling every morning. (In-haling, he said, was easy.) This 'musical exhalation' was made pos-sible by a singularly relaxed technique. Though it also gave rise to some inaccuracies, these in the end mattered little; the gain was over-whelming.

'You're trying too hard!' he would say to highly-strung and self-aware students. But Fischer's influence was not necessarily a relaxing one. He was apt to make the phlegmatic deliberately nervous in order to coax from them a spark of temperament. And he liked to put the pressure on when it was a question of establishing the grand design: he encouraged us not to take things apart and show their components, but to put them together, place them in perspective, and see the detail in the context of the whole.

III

How can I convey the impact of Fischer's playing to someone who never heard him 'live'?

During the nineteen-fifties, an orchestral player once came up to me after a rehearsal. He said he used to play in Edwin Fischer's chamber orchestra, and in his imagination was still doing so. He recalled particularly how fresh the Bach concertos used to sound in each performance. Even now, twenty-five years later, he still had goose-pimples whenever he thought of a certain passage. 'Look at this,' he said, rolling up his sleeve.

Fischer, particularly after the last war, was afraid of the microphone. The recording he made of Brahms's F minor Sonata, for example, gives only one glimpse – at the entry of the D flat major 'patriotic' theme in the last movement – of his real conception of that work. Fortunately, there are among his records some which come fairly close to the reality of his playing. A few even set a standard of unmannered perfection which transcends the bounds of fashion. Best among his earlier records, in my opinion, are a number of wonderful Bach interpretations, as well as the Schubert Impromptus and the Mozart Concertos K 466 (D minor) and K 491 (C minor); among his later ones Bach's C major Concerto for Three Pianos (with Ronald Smith and Denis Matthews) and Beethoven's *Emperor* Concerto under Furtwängler. The recording of Bach's C major Concerto was not done with his usual partners (who were former pupils); all the more admirable, then, is the complete unanimity of style, impressive proof of Fischer's power of communication. His conducting of the tuttis in Beethoven's Third and Fourth Concertos on his post-war records is, to my ears, still unsurpassed. A disc of Schubert Lieder with Elisabeth Schwarzkopf, and the recording of Brahms's G major Violin Sonata with Gioconda de Vito bear eloquent testimony to his mellow late style. The performances of the Fischer Trio unfortunately only live on in the memory of those who were present at their concerts; how could the recording industry possibly have let this happen?

(1976)

COPING WITH PIANOS

COPING WITH PIANOS

I

'There are no bad pianos, only bad pianists.' An impressive state-ment, one that looks round for applause. A statement that will at once ring true to the layman and make him feel initiated as well as amused. A statement addressed perhaps to some revered virtuoso who did not refuse to play at a private party – Busoni would have left the house right away – and who, in spite of the detestable instrument, managed to hold his audience spellbound.

It is a statement to confound any pianist. Admittedly, many a piano will sound less awful under the hands of an expert than under those of an amateur; but does that make it a good piano? To 'carry the day' on a badly regulated, unequally registered, faultily voiced, dull or noisy instrument implies as often as not that one has violated the music for which one is responsible, that control and refinement have been pushed aside, that the 'personal approach' has been greatly exagger-ated and a dubious sort of mystique has taken over, far removed from the effect the piece should legitimately produce.

How often does the player find a piano he can rely on, a piano which will do justice to the exactness of his vision? Is it to be won-dered at that many of his performances remain compromises? After all, he should not have to struggle with the instrument, or impose his will tyrannically upon it, any more than the instrument should turn into a fetish, an object of idolization that dominates him. On the con-trary, the player should make friends with the piano and assure him-self of its services – especially when Pianism with a capital P is to be transcended. He should give the instrument its due by showing how capable it is of transforming itself.

A piano is not a mass-produced article. Every instrument, even from the same renowned maker, presents the pianist with a new experience. What shapes his reaction is not only the 'individuality' of a particular instrument, but also the materials used in it and the processes of manufacture – in other words, the difference in quality between one instrument and another. Enviously he watches the cellist dragging his own cello around; his only consolation is that the adjustment problems of organists and harpsichordists exceed his own. What energy is sometimes needed to 'listen into' a particular piano, and what pertinacity to make it amenable to a certain piece of music! The pianist will find that the instrument readily responds to some pieces, but balks at others. He may, unexpectedly, be reminded of the piano he used in his youth, or on which he studied a certain piece: intention and execution suddenly coalesce once more; something of the joy and concentration of his early strivings comes back to him; old, crumpled fingerings regain their pristine smoothness – it is a homecoming into the lower reaches of memory.

Once in a while a piano will surprise the player by demonstrating to him the nature of the instrument on which a composer conceived a particular work: a piano with a singing tone, a tender treble, gentle bass, and a harp-like, whispering soft pedal will bring Liszt's *Bénédiction* to life, and the lower middle range of a Bösendorfer will remove Schubert's accompaniment figures to their proper distance. A Pleyel upright amidst velvet draperies, cushions, carpets and plush furnishings might perhaps reveal the sense of Chopin's pedal markings. Pianos and rooms are generally interdependent: anyone who has ever travelled with a piano knows that the same Steinway or Bösendorfer not only sounds different in different halls, but also seems to react differently in its mechanism. Indeed, the resistance of the key, over and above the measurable mechanical aspect, is a psychological factor. The characteristics of a concert hall – its greater or lesser resonance, brightness, clarity, and spaciousness of sound – are reflected in the player's technical approach and have an influence on his sense of well-being. There are halls that coarsen or deaden the sound; others absorb one's pedalling like blotting-paper or, conversely, require constant non-legato playing. Thus (to return to Chopin's pedal signs) there can be no universally valid pedalling instructions – these exist only in the imagination of some piano teachers. Excepted, of course, are pedal markings which determine the colour of entire sections, indicate pedal points, or ask for some kind of pedalling which is not self-evident; most of Beethoven's infrequent pedal markings belong in these categories.

Much will depend on the previous concert: are the new hall and instrument reassuringly similar, or will the pianist have to readjust himself? If the latter, his aural and technical reorientation before the concert will have the additional aim of ridding his memory as far as possible of all recently acquired habits of listening and playing. However, the pianist's attempts to adapt himself to instrument and hall are beset by a multitude of difficulties.

In the first place, the full hall during the concert sometimes sounds completely different from the empty one during the rehearsal. The halls of the Vienna Musikverein, for instance, famous for their acoustics, overflow in a welter of sound when empty. (The only time that Viennese orchestral musicians can hear one another at all clearly is during the performance.)

Moreover, the sound reaching the public in the auditorium only rarely corresponds to that heard on the platform. In extreme cases, the player may know perfectly well what is happening on stage, but not at all what is coming across. He must then try to translate his musical intentions into a presumed sound which he himself can control only indirectly. This acoustic equivalent of reading the tea-leaves can at times lead even the most experienced pianist astray. Unless he has sat in the hall himself as a member of the audience and knows exactly what the sound is like from there, the player will have to rely on the advice of musical friends. At recording sessions, the sound of test tapes through the speakers in the playback room will tell him whether and in what proportions he will have to split his musical personality.

Another problem is that, on the rare occasions when he has the luxury of choice, the pianist cannot often compare the available pianos side by side in the hall. He has to go to the storage room of the hall or hiring firm, or encounter each instrument in a different location. The divergent acoustics can widely mislead him in his choice.

Lastly, there is no denying the fact that we pianists do not always 'function like clockwork'. I am referring not only to the changing lubrication level of our physical apparatus, which at times enables us to throw off with the grace of an acrobat what at other times weighs upon us like a ton of bricks; I am referring also to the quality of our hearing, which may vary under the influence of tiredness or freshness, anxiety or repose.

There are some pianists fatalistic enough to assail the platform blissfully unaware. However, they are as rare as albinos. In spite of all the obstacles, the experience gained at the rehearsal will be useful at the performance, even though, as might happen, the pianist may well have to revise his impressions yet again. At any rate, he has over-hauled the instrument with the help of the tuner. He has positioned the piano correctly, not too close to the edge of the platform, the keyboard exactly in the centre of the hall. He has removed the music stand, tried and rejected three piano stools (the fourth, at last, did not creak or wobble), arranged the lighting so that no shadow falling on the keys should disturb his concentration, and located an old upright on which to warm up briefly before facing the audience. He has also, with luck, almost at the back of his mind, recalled the whole pro-gramme he is to play. Now he may sleep through the afternoon.

II

Reactions to a piano are a personal matter; they are not always sharply defined and are subject to continual change. The pianist has to take into account whether he is going to accompany songs or brave the orchestra in the First Bartók Concerto; whether he is to perform before an audience of fifty or five thousand; whether he is to play Schubert or Stravinsky, Beethoven's *Waldstein* Sonata or Beet-hoven's Op. 110. Can one, nevertheless, lay down some general guidelines for the evaluation of an instrument, which could be of assistance to most pianists in most situations? Let me do so by sub-mitting the following propositions:

1) The piano should be dynamically even in all its registers and at all levels of volume. This evenness can only be achieved by careful regulation of the action, together with the technique of voicing, which I shall come back to later.

2) The tone of the piano should be bright and radiant, but have no cutting edge. The rounder, duller, blunter the tone, the less chance one has to colour it, to mix timbres, to detach one layer of sound from another. Faced with the choice between a concert grand with an inhe-rently beautiful but invariable tone, and a less noble but more col-ourful instrument, the pianist will usually prefer the more colourful one.

3) The volume of the piano should range from a whisper to a roar.

This again depends on a carefully regulated action, which does not require the player to possess superhuman strength, and yet is responsive to his control of the most tender *sotto voce*. Furthermore, resounding splendour must be attainable even in passages and trills within the upper middle range without unduly tiring the hand.

4) The sustaining pedal must dampen precisely. Even when lowered quite slowly onto the strings, all dampers must remain completely noiseless. The much feared grinding and soughing of the dampers at the point of contact, a chronic complaint especially in North America, will, as likely as not, be blamed on the pianist as a technical shortcoming. Without properly shaped and regulated dampers made of good felt, refined, atmospheric pedalling is simply impossible. The lever of the pedal should not have too great a degree of play.

5) The tone of the soft pedal, i.e. the depressed left pedal, should not be thin and acid, but should retain sufficient lyrical roundness and plasticity of sound variation.

6) The pitch of the piano should be able to survive a concert without major dislocation. (If a concert grand goes out of tune, the fault often lies not with the instrument, but with the inadequate skill of the tuner.)

Where I expect some disagreement is over the question of the soft pedal. There are pianists who prefer a shallow, nasal *con sordino* tone, decidedly removed from the normal gamut of sound. This 'grotesque' tone can, by virtue of its sharper definition, be of advantage in over-resonant halls. However, it may be so intolerant of nuances that the result is a single, unvaried tone colour. I find this too much of a restriction. Distinct whispering, important as it may be, is after all only a very small part of the musical function of the soft pedal. I recommend three test passages:

a) The A flat major second subject of Schubert's Impromptu Op. 142, No. 1. (Its many repeated *pianissimo* notes, surrounded by a halo of pedal, should retain their singing delicacy without an accumulation of ugly metallic noises and unpredictable 'snarl-ups'.)

b) The high treble trill towards the end of Beethoven's Sonata Op. 111. (Many modern grands turn its atmospheric vibration into an *étude*-like succession of prickly single notes that pierce the ear like tin-tacks.)

c) The first lines of Liszt's *Bénédiction de Dieu dans la Solitude.* (Liszt asks for *mezzoforte* cantilenas in the middle range! The soft pedal sounds should allow plenty of room for dynamic gradations – a reproduction, as it were, of the full volume on a reduced scale. It is wrong to believe that the sordino permits only gentle playing. This assumption had already been contradicted in the *una corda* sections of Beethoven's *Hammerklavier* Sonata.)

The position of the hammers during the depression of the left pedal is regulated by an easily adjustable screw at the right edge of the keyboard. A nasal-sounding sordino can sometimes be corrected by reducing the distance by which the left pedal shifts the action to the right. If, however, the adjustment of the screw has not achieved the desired result, the voicing prong may work wonders by pricking the left outside edge of the hammer heads.

What does the term 'voicing' mean? It refers to the equalization of volume. When whole sections of the keyboard or single notes have become too loud – which happens after virtually every concert – voicing can quickly adapt them again to the general sound level. Notes which are too soft, however, either owing to careless voicing or to defects inherent in the particular instrument, are, in the short term at least, awkward or impossible to deal with. Unfortunately, skilful voicing is rare. The difficulties begin with the prerequisites: the ear must be capable of perceiving the finest gradations of dynamics and timbre; moreover, only a perfectly even *piano legato* touch will reliably show up unevenness of sound. Neither ability can really be expected from a tuner. The smooth, soft *legato* execution of a chromatic scale falls within the province of the professional pianist: it needs regular, attentive practice.

Besides, sensitivity to colour and dynamics is, of course, less highly developed in a tuner than the capacity for distinguishing minute variations in pitch – in this, certainly, he surpasses most pianists. I am well aware that my suggestion to take a *piano legato* touch as one's starting point when testing the evenness of an instrument runs counter to the orthodox method of the technicians. They drop the arm strongly and separately on each key, but in my experience this is of little use in obtaining the subtle distinctions needed in voicing. It does not lead to evenness in the *piano,* let alone the *pianissimo* range. Unevenness of volume is, however, musically more disturbing the softer – and not the louder! – one plays. Solitary rough notes which rear up like mountain peaks from the undulating contours of a *piano* phrase may well pass unnoticed within the towering cliffs of a *forte* phrase. In any case, a good pianist will give a more cragged profile to a *forte* phrase; his declamation will inhabit a wider dynamic space, and the pronounced differences in level intended from one note to the next may well carry the ear across any unintentional accents caused by unsatisfactory voicing.

Only a collaboration between pianist and tuner can achieve the precise voicing of the instrument in all its registers – a view readily endorsed by the most expert piano technicians. I say 'can', for the ignorance of some tuners, even in large cities, in matters of voicing is at times alarming. Time and again I meet concert tuners who do not seem to realize that one must check for evenness of volume separately with and without the left pedal, and that one can use the voicing prong independently in both positions of the action! How to prick the felt of the hammer heads without weakening the basic quality of the tone is another unsolved mystery to most. I should like to put on record here some personal observations on the subject of voicing.

In general I use a voicing instrument with three prongs, in special cases one with a single short prong. The hammer head must never be pierced horizontally – in its effect on tone, this would be like pricking a balloon. Nor is it usually advisable to push vertically into the crown, where the hammer touches the string. One should aim along the crown of the hammer head at a slight angle in the direction of its centre. These thrusts may be deep and forceful. Gentle prickings of the crown itself – exactly vertically into the grooves according to the Bechstein method, or at a right angle to them – will not remain effective for long, but will after a while threaten the tone quality itself. Obtrusive *con sordino* notes are in most cases voiced on the outermost left rim of the hammer head. If this method does not help, the hammer head must be 'auscultated' while the strings are being stopped; it will then become apparent which portion of the hammer head is producing the harsh sound. Sometimes the correct position of the hammer will only be found by moving it to right or left. (If, when the sordino pedal is fully depressed, a single hammer simultaneously strikes two notes, it must be slightly drawn to the left with the help of an adjusting screw.)

Two remarks are frequently made by piano technicians: 'Voicing is a matter of taste,' and 'There's never an end to the job of voicing.' But if one starts from the principle that the brightness of the upper half of a piano should not be reduced except in extreme cases, and if one restricts oneself to the general aim of dynamic evenness, i.e. the adjustment of over-prominent notes or groups of notes to the overall level of sound, then voicing becomes not so much a question of taste as one of skill. Where there is skill, and also sufficient time and patience, one can certainly bring to completion the voicing of a well regulated piano. It is only when the tuner disturbs the core of the tone or overshoots the mark, instead of carefully doing what needs to be done in progressive stages, that he will 'never come to the end of it'. For if he is careless he will be forced, as his work proceeds, to take the notes that have become too soft as a new point of reference, adapting neighbouring notes to their level. Dullness of tone is the likely result.

Piano tuners and technicians should be given every possible encouragement in their profession. Their status and standard of living needs to be improved in many countries; they should be supported by scholarships during their long training period. Today, we have an incomparably larger number of passable pianists than of piano technicians. The few good concert tuners are usually overworked, and after doing their jobs in concert halls, recording studios and radio stations have no time left in which to impart their skill. Some of them anxiously guard their secrets. If only one could make some piano players understand that they would be of greater service to music as piano technicians! The training of the tuner should, in any case, put more emphasis on the artistic education of the ear. And tuners should – in my Utopian view – be better pianists. On the other hand, all pianists should be expert voicers – if only in self-defence. A course on the regulating and voicing of pianos should be obligatory for all piano students at music schools. (An examination in organ building for organ students has already been introduced at some musical institutes.)

Much of the uncertainty and indifference of tuners has its roots in the ignorance of pianists, who are unable to perceive clearly and put into words what worries them about an instrument. Many pianists do not even realize how much they are entitled to expect from a concert grand. It almost seems as if the piano firms turn that ignorance to their advantage and sometimes release from their factories instruments with the most amazing congenital defects or teething troubles. Looked at from this angle, the statement 'There are no bad pianos, only bad pianists' reads like the motto of a piano dealer trying to divert attention from the impending decline in the art of piano building. I have played on brand-new concert grands whose dynamic range in the upper middle register would have been just adequate for accompanying an elderly singer in *Die Winterreise*. I have played on others where whole bundles of notes failed to react to forceful repetition: they just did not work. Many pianos are like unmade beds; a tuner, apart from his actual tuning, will rarely have the initiative to prepare a piano thoroughly for a concert. He will say to himself, 'When the pianist tries it, he will soon tell me what he wants done.' This means that the pianist has to expend precious time on mechanical matters – time he would much rather give to his music, or spend in relaxation, such as taking a walk, visiting a museum, or having a nap. It also means that, considering the shortness of time available and the sorry state in which so many pianos are found, it will be possible to undertake only part of the necessary work. The remaining defects of the instrument will then press upon the pianist during the performance, and he will have to make a conscious effort to ward them off.

III

In the age of the gramophone record, concerts on inadequate pianos make less sense than ever. The player should be given the opportunity of competing with his own recordings. But does he have a chance at all, when the instrument used at the recording sessions is more carefully chosen and kept in better order than is usual for concerts? When the tuner is always in attendance, ready to deal with every crackle, every change in pitch, every loud key? Surely, when there is the possibility to repeat and improve things in the studio, to overcome the fluttering of one's heart, to banish the blind spots of concentration, to commune with oneself in perfect peace, to be undistracted by the coughing fits of the audience – surely all this results in an end product which comes nearer to the player's ideal? And is it not true that the art of the sound engineer, beguiling the ear with the best of all possible piano sounds, makes the listener independent of the acoustic disadvantages of his seat in the concert hall?

Happily for live music-making, the reality is less rosy. In coping with pianos, modern recording technique appears to run into one problem after another. Why was it so easy to make good piano recordings in the nineteen-thirties? When listening to the records of Cortot, Fischer or Schnabel, I feel as if I were sitting in a good seat in a good hall; the timbre of the great pianist is there, the piano sounds homogeneous in all registers, dynamic climaxes and hushed tones come over with equal conviction. And that impression cannot be shaken by technical explanations designed to prove to me that the limitations of early recording techniques did not permit a faithful musical reproduction.

To me, it seems more likely that with the over-refinements of modern techniques one is apt to miss the wood for the trees. Thus, certain discs nowadays need very special speakers, which, in turn, have to be placed in the right sort of room for the sound to acquire its proper physical consistency – for otherwise the treble and bass of the piano may split apart as if coming from different instruments or different distances. While the engineers of the old 78-r.p.m. days may still in all innocence have heard the music as a horizontal succession of sounds, their present-day colleagues, with their imposing musical and technical qualifications, have difficulty in breaking away from the habit of vertical listening, the close scrutinizing of knife-edge synchronization of sounds, which the modern practice of tape editing has inculcated in them as second nature.

And what about the artist's self-communings in splendid, peaceful isolation? Is he really impervious to the malice of the instrument, the touchiness of the equipment, the host of possible noises? Does not every visit to the playback room cut off his physical contact with the piano? Does a concert pianist actually want to soliloquize? – surely only when the composer seems to wish him to do so, as in some of Beethoven's slow movements, where the music withdraws into an inner world. And even here the player's approach is conditioned by his intention to let himself be overheard; even a whispered utterance, an aside, must remain intelligible to the audience. This illusion of the listener being admitted to the player's confidence becomes a moving experience in the concert hall. The individual listener is picked out: the player favours him with his inmost secrets. This shrinking of the distance between audience and platform is an achievement which should never be taken for granted; the player has to work for it. In front of the loudspeakers, the listener's privilege turns into stale reality; he is alone with his gramophone in any case, and he can, if he is so inclined, overhear the 'secret' at double the volume: it will lie before him, huge and penetrating, within arm's reach. The recorded performance does not depend for its success upon the listener's concentrated attention. It has already happened and now rolls along without any contribution from him, until he turns off the machine. In the concert hall, each motionless listener is part of the performance. The concentration of the player charges the electric tension in the auditorium and returns to him magnified; thus the audience makes its contribution, helping the pianist to cope with his instrument. At home, in front of his stereo equipment, the ideal listener will strive to attain a similar state of concentration, drawing on his experience of past concerts – just as the pianist did when he played in the recording studio for an imaginary audience.

(1974)

TALKING TO BRENDEL

TALKING TO BRENDEL
Jeremy Siepmann

JEREMY
SIEPMANN

This may seem an odd sort of question to be asking you, but I know enough about performers to know that the answer is by no means a foregone conclusion: do you enjoy performing?

ALFRED
BRENDEL

Yes. Yes, I do. I've enjoyed it particularly during the last few years, when I've had the impression that much of what I do comes across. Of course, one very rarely knows if the right things come across; I collect tapes of my concert performances to check what I've done, but the sound captured by the microphone may be quite different from the sound in the twenty-third row.

SIEPMANN

Not to mention the *meaning* of the sound, which may vary in as many degrees as there are seats in the twenty-third row. Does it disturb you that musical communication can't be more precise?

BRENDEL

Yes. A lot of it disturbs me. Even the appreciation of the audience disturbs me sometimes, because it appreciates good things and bad nearly alike. Although one is extremely dependent on an audience's appreciation, because one has to convey a message, one must try, if it is possible, to remain completely independent of other people's judgements.

SIEPMANN   You say that an audience may appreciate something which is 'bad', yet what is bad to one listener may be good to another equally qualified to form a judgement. Do you think that there *is* a distinct Right and Wrong, a distinct Good and Bad, in musical performance? Or does it in the end, beyond a certain level of professional attainment, boil down to personal preference, resulting from a particular psychological or spiritual bent?

BRENDEL   To a certain extent it does, yes; but maybe not entirely. If one takes as a basis of judgement a very high professional level, and a real knowledge of the music involved – knowledge born from talent, from experience, and informed by psychological insight into what happens in a piece of music – then one gets nearer, I think, to judgements which are not so opposed.

SIEPMANN   You've said that performers exist to be a link between the composer and the audience. That's true, of course, but is it as simple as that?

BRENDEL   No. I must say that I myself am far more interested in the relation to the composer than in the relation towards the public. What fascinates me is to make sense of a piece of music while it sounds. That I convey something to the public is partly a necessary evil, but it's also a wonderful challenge. I say it's an evil because it may give the performer feelings of power which oughtn't to come into it. He may so enjoy having a hold over his audience that he forgets what he's for as a musician. Musical values and a performer's grip on his audience aren't always quite the same thing!

SIEPMANN   Is it a performer's job to 'teach' his audience? I remember hearing a distinguished performer who'd been asked if he would bring out each appearance of the subject in a fugue. He said, in effect, 'Not when I'm playing it for myself. I know it's there. I can see it; I can hear it; I can even feel it. But in a concert I would.' To what extent do you think this double standard is justified?

BRENDEL   There are two points. First of all, the performer has to
           clarify a piece, to make it as clearly accessible as pos-
           sible. Listening should always be made easy, whether
           it's to late Beethoven quartets or Mozart sonatas.
           There should be a blend of the performer's feeling and
           the music which doesn't give the impression that
           there's any great strain involved. The second point is
           that the moment an audience feels that a performer
           wants to teach them, his case is lost. If you teach an
           audience, they mustn't ever notice it.

SIEPMANN   Do you think musical analysis is of any value to the
           performer as a performer?

BRENDEL   I think every performer should have a sound back-
           ground as a composer, and know enough about tradi-
           tional harmony and counterpoint so that it won't give
           him much trouble to write a cadenza which is without
           obvious faults of voice-leading [part-writing] and so
           on. As for analysis, there are many ways of analysing
           music, some more helpful to performers than others.
           But it's interesting to note that composers have rarely
           spoken at all about musical analysis. They've avoided
           the subject to an extent which seems to me very re-
           vealing. One finds, on the other hand, a lot of comment
           about atmosphere, about character, about poetic ideas
           – even in the most unlikely places. Performers who
           nourish poetic ideas are excused by the composers
           themselves. Analysis should never be taken for the key
           to the sort of insight which enables a great perfor-
           mance. If we know that there is an extremely important
           harmonic progression – if, for instance, we analyse a
           piece in Schenker's way – and we do not feel, while we
           are playing it, the exact amount of tension, the way
           atmosphere changes at this point, the balance of all the
           elements involved, then our knowledge will help us not
           at all. It was Schoenberg who said, in a letter, that
           formal analysis is often overrated because it shows *how*
           something is done, not *what* is done. This, from one of
           the supreme analysts, is something valuable, I think.

SIEPMANN   Do you think live and recorded performances encourage, or perhaps even require, different approaches to listening? The very nature of a recording, after all, is unnatural (even, arguably, unmusical) in that in life a performance is never repeated time and again without change. Does this require us to adjust our attitudes?

BRENDEL   There are, certainly, basic differences; but after fifty or sixty records I'm still not able to cite them all! When I made my first records I decided that a recorded performance was something quite different, in that one doesn't see the performer and that, for the performer, there is no audience. What counted was the result (the edited tape), not the risk. But the more I progressed in recording experience, the more I tried to play as though in a concert, imagining that an audience was there, listening to me. I came to this after listening to tapes from my own concerts and comparing them with some of my records. Many more concerts, I think, should be recorded and issued on disc, with all their imperfections and coughing and so on. As far as piano recordings are concerned, the over-refinement of our tools nowadays seems sometimes to be a disadvantage.

SIEPMANN   Do you consciously alter the details of a performance for a recording?

BRENDEL   I do not – unless when I listen to the playback I find that something sounds out of proportion and wouldn't have the same impact as when one could see me, or feel my bodily presence in a hall.

SIEPMANN   Do you feel, as I would gather you do, that there is a musical function in the gestures a performer makes? That he can, or even should, use his physical presence to support or draw attention to certain moments in the music?

BRENDEL   Yes, I do. When I saw myself on television for the first time, I became aware that I'd developed all kinds of gestures and grimaces which completely contradicted what I did, and what, musically, I wanted to do. I then had a mirror made, a big standing mirror, which I put beside the piano, not really making me visible all the time, but always there; unconsciously, one noticed things. It helped me to co-ordinate what I wanted to suggest with my movements with what really came out. There are many examples of pieces where this is necessary. Things like the end of Liszt's B minor Sonata, where before the three *pianississimo* B major chords there is a crescendo on one chord which one has to convey bodily, with a gesture. It's the only possibility.

SIEPMANN   You've made an enormous number of records over the years. What is your relationship to all these progeny?

BRENDEL   Records are a kind of offspring of which one can't, unfortunately, say that one has to nurse them until they grow up and then forget them as soon as possible and let them lead their own lives. They lead their own lives at once, and are scarcely ever grown up! There's always something infantile about a record, at least as far as the artist is concerned. Records are interesting to learn from – but not always to enjoy.

SIEPMANN   What do you think has been the effect on general musical life of the advent of the gramophone and the radio, and the easy accessibility of music which it has brought? Certainly it seems to have greatly diminished the amount of amateur music-making.

BRENDEL   Yes, which I think is a great pity. On the other hand, it has enabled so many more people and classes to participate in the enjoyment of music. It's now much less the privilege of, financially speaking, the upper classes.

SIEPMANN   This touches on a question which interests me very much. Is there, do you think, any inherently *musical* reason why so-called 'serious' music should be, should have been, the province, generally, of the aristocracy, the intelligentsia, the educated middle or upper-middle classes, and why it seems to exert less appeal to 'the common man' than pop, jazz or musical comedy?

BRENDEL   One of the obvious reasons is that the common man has
           no background in his youth which leads him to
           appreciate this music, or very much less than other
           social classes. I think there are a great many social bar-
           riers still to come down before we can have any clear
           answer to this question.

SIEPMANN   Have you any ideas as to how to bring them down?
           There is, after all, what with radio and the
           gramophone, an enormous amount of serious music
           available, and easily accessible, to a very great range of
           people. How does one see to it that it does become a
           part of their background? Or ought one not to try?

BRENDEL   I certainly wouldn't want to force it down anybody's
           throat. It is nice, sometimes, to know that there are
           some reserves, some pieces of music, which stay nearly
           inaccessible to so many people. But it matters so much
           what you learn at school, and I think the training and
           the kind of stimulation which you get at schools seems
           completely inadequate in most places.

SIEPMANN   I've read that you're interested in writing about music.

BRENDEL   Yes.

SIEPMANN   As you've seen, one of the questions I've written down
           is 'Is music a subject to be written about?' Presumably
           your answer is yes, in certain circumstances and by cer-
           tain people.

BRENDEL   Yes. Yes. I think one should sometimes try to do the
           impossible!

SIEPMANN   What can, or should, writing about music achieve, and,
           if you like, what must it not try to achieve?

BRENDEL   First of all, I think it must not be arrogant. That may
           seem very irrelevant, but I think it's very important. If
           one decides to talk about something as elusive as music,
           something which is so difficult to grasp in words
           without talking nonsense all the time and being impre-
           cise to an enormous degree, and personal to a degree
           which is no use to anyone, then one has to be modest

about it. I haven't read many books on music which
were worth reading once the purely historical and bio-
graphical material ended and the analysis, the attempt
to illuminate something about music, began.

SIEPMANN   Your own extra-musical interests are wide-ranging. Do
you think that a knowledge of other arts, such as
painting, architecture, literature, etc., and acquain-
tance with other spiritual-cum-intellectual pursuits
such as philosophy, can affect a musician *as a musician*? And would you recommend the study of them to
those not naturally drawn to them?

BRENDEL   One can only answer questions like these for oneself.
For me it definitely has. It's all part of my aesthetic
food, really. I wouldn't feel properly fed without it, but
I wouldn't necessarily recommend it to others. After
all, there are enormously talented musicians who are
completely unvisual, even colour-blind. What I *would*
recommend, to all musicians, is to see what is happening around them, to face reality and not to take any
of the many, many ways of escape which people so
often do; I doubt if there have ever been so many problems of such actuality, in the whole history of mankind,
as there are today. If people would face the reality, then
one could do something about it. But it would change
their lives. Our lives.

SIEPMANN   Do you see dangers in the concept of 'music as refuge'?

BRENDEL   It can be a refuge, certainly. Music can be so many
things. It can lift one into a sphere which is remote from
time, and from reality. That is one of music's marvellous possibilities. But it's not the only one.

SIEPMANN   I've read that amongst your many interests is the study
of Baroque architecture, but I think I'm right in saying
that you rarely, if ever, include Baroque music in your
programmes. Do you ever play music which was
written for the harpsichord?

BRENDEL   Virtually never.[1]

[1] This statement was made in 1972. My outlook since then has changed.

SIEPMANN   Why?

BRENDEL   It's a very personal question, really. One of the reasons, certainly, is the use of the instrument – though I don't object to someone who manages to play Bach convincingly on the piano. Unlike Scarlatti, which I cannot bear to hear on the piano.

SIEPMANN   No matter who plays it?

BRENDEL   No matter who plays it. In comparison with an excellent performance on the harpsichord, this music makes no sense to me at all on the piano. But there is some of the old English music – the Fantasia by Gibbons in *Parthenia*, for example – which I think is better suited to the piano than to many of the old instruments, because it is so madrigal-like. It is music of singing voices, of sustained sound.

SIEPMANN   What are your feelings about what I call 'reconstructionist' performances, in which musicians aim to recapture precisely the style and sound of music as it was in the days of the composer? Do you think it's possible, with all our subsequent musical experience, to recapture that? We can perhaps reconstruct the sound, but can we recapture the experience? And is it worth trying?

BRENDEL   It certainly seems to be worth trying. Because even if it doesn't recapture the experience as a whole, the sound has a strong bearing on the quality of the experience. The timbre of some of the instruments involved, and the way of treating the music which these instruments suggest, may have very great significance. For instance, take Monteverdi – hearing the actual instruments of his time, even if we don't know exactly how they were used, makes all the difference to me. Especially after so many transcriptions by Hindemith and Malipiero and God knows who. I listen with completely new ears. Now with piano music . . . .

SIEPMANN   In Mozart concertos, for instance, to what extent do you try to tailor your playing on a modern concert grand to the ideal of the Mozartian piano sound?

BRENDEL   I think of the whole piece, and of all the players involved. As I don't play with players who use old instruments, it would make little sense for me to try and adjust my playing to an old instrument. For myself, I find it much more interesting and important to make as much as I can of the present-day piano, to make the limits wider and wider in every respect. I try to see each work as a problem by itself – less an historical than a psychological problem, a problem of character.

SIEPMANN   In view of the widespread availability of what I shall call 'mainstream' performances, do you think there is any justification for the attempts of certain players to shed new light or encourage a new way of listening to the extent that they deliberately distort, or, if you like, pervert the composer's markings?

BRENDEL   It depends on the way in which one wants to shed new light. I think, actually, that the attempt to do it is wrong in the first place. If one sheds new light on music, it should be the *outcome* of an effort, not the input! As is originality. If one sets out to be original, especially as a performer, one is bound to get lost. Indeed, if one sets out with that aim it's likely that one has very little talent in the first place. If one alters a composer's markings in order to be interesting, then one is simply foolish. But it's fascinating to see that quite a lot of people are attracted by this approach and seem even to find it intellectually justified.

SIEPMANN   Do you make a point of keeping abreast of contemporary music?

BRENDEL   Yes, I do. I haven't enough time to do it as I would like, but I go whenever I can to listen, at the Round House or wherever.

SIEPMANN   Do you feel, as a performer, any obligation to contemporary composers?

BRENDEL   No, I must admit I do not. But I feel that they ought to be encouraged. I don't play them because I would have to specialize completely in a certain field of music in order to do it really well. I would have to confine myself to a rather limited number of works instead of playing an enormous repertoire, and I decided otherwise.

SIEPMANN   Do you, on the whole, learn quickly?

BRENDEL   Yes. I haven't got a visual memory. My memory isn't phenomenal, but it's quite good on the whole.

SIEPMANN   Is your memory extremely retentive, or do you have to keep re-learning?

BRENDEL   I have to keep re-learning – which is, I think, a very good thing. It makes for many new encounters and never allows one to feel unduly secure in reproducing some old hat!

SIEPMANN   Do you ever feel the necessity to get right away from music for a time, to go away from the piano and away from where you hear music?

BRENDEL   Each year, for about two weeks, at the beginning of my vacation, I don't touch the instrument. And while I may hear music, I don't plan or expect to. I like to look at architecture and to drive around. And every four or five years I try to take off a period of some months which I devote completely to study, and maybe sometimes to recording as well.

SIEPMANN   Do you ever feel a temptation to branch out? To conduct, perhaps?

BRENDEL   I'm very interested in conducting, and in the techniques of conducting. I imagine myself conducting, but I would never do it. I am interested in the piano. I think I would be too shy to attempt to impose something on an orchestra without being completely professional. However well I know a piece, and what the orchestra can do, there would always be a gap between my standard as a pianist and my standard as a conductor.

SIEPMANN   You are now a very successful concert performer. Should success grant you the freedom to order your professional life precisely as you see fit, what changes, if any, would you be tempted to make?

BRENDEL   I don't know. So far I don't feel at all exploited. I play a lot, though not as much as some other people, but I play because I like it. I have a lot of other interests, of course, for which time will always be too short. But there it is.

APPENDIX:

The Process of Foreshortening in the First Movement of Beethoven's Sonata Op. 2, No. 1

In my essay 'Form and Psychology in Beethoven's Piano Sonatas' I mentioned that the opening theme of the Sonata Op. 2, No. 1 consisted of two two-bar units, two one-bar units and three half-bar units leading to a fermata (see example on p.42). The next six bars foreshorten the eight-bar opening. First we have two bars of C minor harmony, in which a fourth crotchet is added to the melody at the end of the triplet turn.

This crotchet leads on from where the phrases of the theme had previously broken off, and enhances the intensity by repetition. The next four bars bring fragmentation:

In the first two bars the upper two voices imitate the final fragment of the theme; in the last two only the 'soprano' has the fragment and the harmonies follow each other more closely. (While in bars 11/12 the harmonies are still connected by appoggiaturas, bars 13 and 14 have separate harmonic weight.)

In the next six bars (15-20) the sound is smoothed out further. One could say that between bars 9 and 20 the staccato and separate melodic units of the theme have been gradually transformed into legato and continuity. Syncopation is introduced into the melody.

We hear two different subdivisions at the same time: minim (left hand) and crotchet (left plus right). A statement repeated twice with more and more emphasis arouses expectations. The omission of the *crescendo-diminuendo* sign in bar 19 conveys the message that the syncopation is no longer a major event. The crotchet rhythm now dominates, helped by a *forte* marking and octave doublings.

This crotchet rhythm leads into the left-hand quavers of bar 20 ff. These quavers are, however, a case of Dr Jekyll and Mr Hyde: their detailed intensity soon gives way to the impression of a sustained pedal point. And they prove to be disguised two-part writing: the bass carries on the preceding minims, now foreshortened into crotchets,

while the middle voice can be understood as syncopated quavers.

If we play the left hand in a simplified manner, we notice at once how the foreshortenings are organized.

Schematically we have the *ostinato* first:

The bass now starts to move, while the pedal point is retained.

It then moves more quickly, tying pairs of harmonies together.

The last three harmonies stand separate.

What happened in the right hand after bar 20? The seemingly new melodic idea in A flat is in fact related to the first subject as a free inversion.

It insists on making its statement three times. (The second section, beginning at bar 20, is indeed full of repeated notes and phrases.) During the third statement, however, the bass line starts to move and the statement remains unfinished. The right hand now breaks up into ascending syncopations.

From bar 27, where the left hand is further subdivided, the figurated syncopations of the right hand give way to exclamations in which each note has melodic importance; these exclamatory groups are also dynamically emphasized.

During the further harmonic subdivision in which the left-hand harmonies stand separate (bars 31/32) instead of being linked in groups of two (bars 28-31), the right hand is again split up in ascending syncopations, and the left hand underlines their emphasis with four E flats, thus linking the changing harmonies. The ascending syncopations lead to a new idea which transforms the broken-up fragments of melody into a continuous flow of quavers. We now have two sets of four bars of similar construction. Each of the four-bar phrases contains foreshortening: in the first, as a point of departure, we have two bars of descending scale,

then one figuration of the E flat,

and finally two figurations of the E flat.

The foreshortening of the second phrase will be understood in conjunction with the left hand.

In bar 33 the left hand had introduced syncopations. (Even though the value of the notes is much greater than in the preceding bars, the syncopations have a marked effect within the foreshortening process. Here, their importance is stressed by *sforzandi*.) In bars 36 and 40 the syncopations give way to crotchets.

Whereas from bar 33 onwards the harmonies have moved bar by bar, from bar 42 they start to change twice in a bar. During the closing idea (bars 42-49) the syncopated chords of the left hand help to indicate the exalted intensity of feeling (*con espressione*).

The right hand makes three nearly identical statements, the last of which rises to a higher register of the piano and culminates in a *fortissimo* chord. This chord derives additional impact from the fact that it is a dissonance and a kind of written-out fermata.

The development (bar 49 ff.) starts a new foreshortening process. Its first fourteen bars relate to the opening twenty-seven bars of the movement. The exposition of the first theme is now condensed into six bars in two units of three, each of which is subdivided into two plus one, again a foreshortening.

In the second unit the left hand abandons its comparatively passive role to take the initiative: the crotchets lead into a quaver rhythm of broken octaves while the right hand, instead of rising one step, insistently repeats its fragment of the theme at the same pitch, thus increasing the tension.

Beethoven has also written a *crescendo* sign. (Even in his early works, dynamic markings are usually tied to structural events.)

The three-bar units are now succeeded by the two-bar units of the second idea. Bars 55-62 are directly related to bars 20-27. In bars 61/62 the player has to be aware of the rhythmic subdivisions that are required.

When the pedal point on F in the middle voice is abandoned, each of the quavers is given equal importance.

The following five-bar unit (63-67) relates to the foregoing eight-bar phrase, but omits its fragmented ending. The insistent melody moves from the soprano into the bass, signifying an increase of tension.

Three-part writing turns into four-part: there is the added excitement of the right-hand interjections

which greatly influence the further course of the development. They appear split up in syncopations in bars 73-80,

while the left hand strips away the insistent melodic idea: only an

octave skeleton in syncopations remains. In the last bar the motion
has narrowed down to a familiar rhythmic figure:

We recognize the opening theme's accompaniment. This rhythm is
pursued in the middle voice of the left hand,

while the lower voice persists on the dominant in fast syncopations – a
foreshortened consequence of the preceding syncopated minim
rhythm. The melodic line of the middle voice is foreshortened,

and the corresponding foreshortenings in the right hand are easy to
detect. The middle voice leads into repeated notes (bar 93); they
bring continuity to the flow of crotchets which has so far been
inconsistent in both the preceding melodic voices. In spite of the very
low dynamic level, the rhythmic intensity of each repeated note commands our attention.

But again Jekyll turns into Hyde. The introduction of a second and third voice in bar 95 changes the hearing pattern; we now perceive two extended beats per bar rather than four. And the platform of the first two bars, 93/94, gives way to descending bar-by-bar steps in the overlapping voices. The interjections of the right hand are reminiscences of the fierce syncopations (bar 73 ff.) which precede the little thunderstorm in the development. At the same time, they prepare the recapitulation: we know these triplet turns from the initial theme. The left hand also paves the way for the recapitulation; its three-voiced chords in bar 100 foreshadow the accompaniment of the theme and bring back the impact of the crotchet rhythm. The theme, after such masterly introduction, appears with overwhelming self-confidence. All reminders of conventional grace are swept away in the bars that follow, where the left-hand chords are firmly placed on the beat.

This simple firmness after so much syncopation is marvellously effective. Even the anguished question at the end of the theme (bar 8) is turned into defiance in bar 108.

The rest of the movement proceeds on the lines of the exposition. Broadly speaking, the movement consists of two foreshortening series; the first extends from the beginning to the development, the second from the development to the end.

SELECTED BIBLIOGRAPHY

In compiling this list I have concentrated on writings which are quoted or mentioned in the book, or which have a direct bearing on it. I have not included those writings already identified in the text.

BEETHOVEN

Birnbach, Heinrich. 'Über die verschiedene Form grösserer Instrumentaltonstücke aller Art und deren Bearbeitung.' *Berliner Allgemeine Musikalische Zeitung,* 1827.

Cooper, Martin. *Beethoven – The Last Decade, 1817-1827.* Oxford University Press, London, 1970.

Fischer, Edwin. *Ludwig van Beethovens Klaviersonaten.* Insel Verlag, Wiesbaden, 1956.
English edition: *Beethoven's Pianoforte Sonatas.* Translated by Stanley Godman with the collaboration of Paul Hamburger. Faber & Faber, London, 1959.

Lenz, Wilhelm von. *Beethoven et ses trois styles.* St Petersburg, 1852; Paris, 1855; new edition: Legouix, Paris, 1909.

—— *Beethoven – Eine Kunststudie.* Hoffmann & Campe, Hamburg, 1855-60.

Marx, Adolph Bernhard. *Die Lehre von der musikalischen Komposition.* Leipzig, 1838.

Morgenstern, Christian. Poem 'Die unmögliche Tatsache' from 'Palmström' in *Alle Galgenlieder.* Bruno Cassirer, Berlin, 1932.
The end of the poem, in its German text, reads:
'Und er kommt zu dem Ergebnis:
Nur ein Traum war das Erlebnis,
Weil, so schliesst er messerscharf,
Nicht sein *kann,* was nicht sein *darf.*'

Nagel, Wilibald. *Beethoven und seine Klaviersonaten.* 2 vols. Beyer & Söhne, Langensalza, 1923.

Nottebohm, Gustav. *Beethoveniana.* 2 vols. Peters, Leipzig, 1867.

Prod'homme, Jacques-Gabriel. *Les Sonates pour Piano de Beethoven.* Delagrave, Paris, 1936/51.
German edition: *Die Klaviersonaten Beethovens.* Breitkopf & Härtel, Wiesbaden, 1948.

Ratz, Erwin. *Einführung in die musikalische Formenlehre.* Österreichischer Bundesverlag, Vienna, 1951; third edition: Universal Edition, Vienna, 1973.

Riemann, Hugo. *Ludwig van Beethovens sämtliche Klavier-Solosonaten.* Max Hesse, Berlin, 1918/19.

Ries, Ferdinand, and F. G. Wegeler. *Biographische Notizen über Ludwig van Beethoven.* Koblenz, 1838; reprint: Schuster & Loeffler, Berlin, 1906.

Ritzel, Fred. *Die Entwicklung der 'Sonatenform' im musiktheoretischen Schrifttum des 18. und 19. Jahrhunderts.* Breitkopf & Härtel, Wiesbaden, 1968.

Rosenberg, Richard. *Die Klaviersonaten Ludwig van Beethovens.* Urs Graf Verlag, Olten and Lausanne, 1957.

Schenker, Heinrich. *Beethoven – Die letzten Sonaten, Erläuterungs-Ausgaben.* Universal Edition, Vienna.

Schindler, Anton. *Biographie von Ludwig van Beethoven. Münster,* 1840.
English edition: *Beethoven as I knew him.* Edited by D. W. MacArdle. Translated by C. S. Jolly. Faber & Faber, London, 1966.

Schmalenbach, Werner. 'Das Museum ist kein Luxus.' *Frankfurter Allgemeine Zeitung,* 3/4 August 1968.

Tovey, Donald Francis. *A Companion to Beethoven's Pianoforte Sonatas.* The Associated Board of the Royal Schools of Music, London, 1931.
—— *Beethoven.* Oxford University Press, London, 1944.

SCHUBERT

Badura-Skoda, Paul. 'Fehlende Takte und korrumpierte Stellen in klassischen Meisterwerken.' *Neue Zeitschrift für Musik,* Mainz, November 1958.

Brown, Maurice J. E. *Schubert – A Critical Biography.* Macmillan, London, 1958.

—— *Essays on Schubert.* Macmillan, London, 1966.

Cone, Edward T. 'Schubert's Beethoven.' *The Musical Quarterly,* New York, October 1970.

Deutsch, Otto Erich. *Schubert Thematic Catalogue.* J. M. Dent & Sons, London, 1951.

—— *Schubert – A Documentary Biography.* Translated by Eric Blom. J. M. Dent & Sons, London, 1947.

German edition: *Schubert – Die Dokumente seines Lebens.* VEB Deutscher Verlag für Musik, Leipzig, and Bärenreiter Verlag, Kassel, 1964.

Nägeli, Hans Georg. *Vorlesungen über Musik.* Stuttgart and Tübingen, 1826.

Reed, John. *Schubert – The Final Years.* Faber & Faber, London, 1972.

Rosen, Charles. *The Classical Style.* Faber & Faber, London, 1971.

Schnabel, Artur. 'The Piano Sonatas of Franz Schubert.' *The Musical Courier,* New York, 1928. (Mentioned in César Saerchinger, *Artur Schnabel – A Biography,* Cassell & Co., London, 1957.)

LISZT

Fay, Amy. *Music Study in Germany.* Macmillan, London, 1885.

Friedheim, Arthur. *Life and Liszt.* Taplinger, New York, 1961.

Göllerich, August. *Franz Liszt.* Marquardt & Co., Berlin, 1908.

Gottschalg, A. W. *Franz Liszt in Weimar und seine letzten Lebensjahre.* Arthur Glaue, Berlin, 1910.

Jerger, Wilhelm. *Franz Liszts Klavierunterricht von 1884-1886, dargestellt an den Tagebuchaufzeichnungen von August Göllerich.* Gustav Bosse, Regensburg, 1975.

Kodály, Zoltán. *Folk Music of Hungary.* Barrie & Jenkins, London, 1971.

Pfeiffer, Theodor, and Jose Vianna da Motta. *Studien bei Hans von Bülow.* Friedrich Luckhardt, Berlin, 1894.

Searle, Humphrey. *The Music of Liszt.* Williams & Norgate, London, 1954.

Siloti, Alexander. *My Memories of Liszt.* Breitkopf & Härtel, London.

Stradal, August. *Erinnerungen an Franz Liszt.* Paul Haupt, Berne and Leipzig, 1929.

BUSONI

Busoni, Ferruccio. *Entwurf einer neuen Ästhetik der Tonkunst* [first published 1907] *Mit Anmerkungen von Arnold Schoenberg und einem Nachwort von H. H. Stuckenschmidt.* Suhrkamp, Frankfurt, 1974.
American edition: *Sketch of a new Esthetic of Music.* Translated by T. S. Baker. Schirmer, New York, 1911.
—— *Wesen und Einheit der Musik.* Max Hesse, Berlin, 1956.
—— *Busoni – Briefe an seine Frau.* Rotapfel Verlag, Erlenbach, 1935.
English edition: *Busoni – Letters to his Wife.* Translated by Rosamond Ley. Edward Arnold, London, 1938.
Dent, Edward J. *Ferruccio Busoni – A Biography.* Oxford University Press, London, 1933; reprint: Eulenburg, London, 1974.
Pfitzner, Hans. 'Futuristengefahr' in *Gesammelte Schriften I.* Augsburg, 1926-29.
Selden-Goth, Gisella. *Ferruccio Busoni.* E. P. Tal & Co., Leipzig-Vienna-Zürich, 1922.
Stuckenschmidt, H. H. *Ferruccio Busoni – Zeittafel eines Europäers.* Atlantis Verlag, Zürich, 1967.
English edition: *Ferruccio Busoni – Chronicle of a European.* Translated by Sandra Morris. Calder & Boyars, London, 1970.

EDWIN FISCHER

Fischer, Edwin. *Musikalische Betrachtungen.* Tschudy Verlag, St Gallen, 1949.
English edition: *Reflections on Music.* Williams & Norgate, London, 1951.
—— *Von den Aufgaben des Musikers.* Insel Verlag, Wiesbaden, 1960.
Dank an Edwin Fischer. F. A. Brockhaus, Wiesbaden, 1962.
Polgar, Alfred. *Ja und Nein – Schriften des Kritikers.* 4 vols. Rowohlt, Berlin, 1926 etc.

TALKING TO BRENDEL

Schoenberg, Arnold. *Briefe.* B. Schott's Söhne, Mainz, 1958.
English edition: *Letters.* Selected and edited by Erwin Stein. Translated by Eithne Wilkins and Ernst Kaiser. Faber & Faber, London, 1964.

INDEX